YOUR
SHORT GAME
SOLUTION

YOUR **SHORT GAME** SOLUTION

MASTERING THE FINESSE GAME FROM **120 YARDS AND IN**

JAMES SIECKMANN

WITH **DAVID DENUNZIO**

PHOTOGRAPHY BY **ANGUS MURRAY**

AVERY

an imprint of Penguin Random House

New York

an imprint of Penguin Random House LLC
375 Hudson Street
New York, New York 10014

Previously published in hardcover by Gotham Books
Copyright © 2015 by James Sieckmann
Original photography copyright © 2015 by Angus Murray

Most Avery books are available at special quantity discounts for bulk purchase for sales promotions,
premiums, fund-raising, and educational needs. Special books or book excerpts also can be created
to fit specific needs. For details, write SpecialMarkets@penguinrandomhouse.com.

Library of Congress Cataloging-in-Publication Data

Sieckmann, James.
Your short game solution : mastering the finesse game from 120 yards and in / James Sieckmann with
David DeNunzio ; photography by Angus Murray. — First edition.
p.   cm.
ISBN 978-1-592-40906-8
1. Short game (Golf).   2. Golfers—Training of.   I. DeNunzio, David.   II. Murray, Angus, ill.
III. Title.
GV979.S54S58   2015   2014023185
796.3523—dc23

Printed in the United States of America
5   7   9   10   8   6   4

For the love of my life,
MICHELE,
who has sacrificed much and
been unrelenting
in her support.

CONTENTS

ACKNOWLEDGMENTS

I owe much to many, and I'm supremely grateful to all those who have supported and believed in me over the years. First to my father, Whitey, an amazing athlete, tireless worker and devoted husband, who led by example and kept our family close together. To my mother, Lonnie, who taught me to love the game of golf and always thought of her boys before she thought of herself.

Thank you to my brother, Tom, who included me as much as he could during his playing days on the PGA Tour. Not many people would welcome their little brother into the arena as they competed in the U.S. Open and the Masters. Tom, those were amazing days for me, and I wish I could go back and live them again with you.

To my first professional client, Tom Pernice Jr., whose golf knowledge and work ethic are legendary. Your generous support and loyalty over the past two decades have been immeasurable. I've never met a man with a bigger heart or a willingness to go out of his way to help others.

To Dr. Greg Rose and my other Tour clients, whose belief in me as a coach inspires me daily to keep learning, dig deeper, and do my best. To my boss, Steve Shanahan, who taught me how to work hard and pay attention to the details.

Lastly, a big thank you to two real pros: photographer Angus Murray and my editor, David DeNunzio, who despite his busy duties as instruction editor at *Golf* magazine, graciously offered his time, expertise, and experience in the writing of this book.

FOREWORD

A the Titleist Performance Institute (T.P.I.), we use the latest technology to unlock the secrets of the swing, then use what we learn to help our Tour staff professionals squeeze out every ounce of scoring potential from their game. We often do this with state-of-the-art fitness training. Other times, we crunch data. And on some days we go the old-fashioned route and dig it out of the T.P.I. practice-range dirt.

The biggest perk at T.P.I. is getting to work with the biggest names in golf. I see dozens of Titleist staffers every month from all of the tours. One of the most fun to be with is Tom Pernice Jr. Tom is obviously a solid player with multiple wins on both the PGA and Champions tours and he controls his wedges like no player I have ever seen. In my mind he is the best wedge player alive. Obviously, he has the right information on how to hit wedge shots, so when another Titleist player began struggling with his short game, I called Tom and asked if he wouldn't mind helping me out. I knew it was a strange request, especially since I was asking him to share his insights with a competitor. He asked me who the player was, and when I told him it was Ben Crane, he quickly agreed to help. Turns out that Tom and Ben are good friends.

With a few simple setup changes and a key technical alteration, Tom got Ben pitching the ball better than ever. We visited Tom on two other occasions over the next several months: once to help Ben's bunker swing, and another to improve his play from Bermuda lies. When we rang Tom a fourth time, I detected a noticeable pause on the other end of the line. "Guys," said Tom, "I'm more than happy to keep helping you, but why don't you just make an appointment with my short-game coach and have *all* of your questions answered?"

Ben and I looked at each other with surprise and in unison said, "You have a short-game coach?" And that was the first time I heard the name James Sieckmann. It was a day I would never forget, because James has become a close friend and a secret weapon for my players and me.

James was the first coach to explain to me, in simple words, how a short-game swing was completely different from a full swing. Like almost everyone else, I thought the former was just a miniature version of the latter. Was I ever wrong! James's theories made me look at golf in a completely different light and answered questions about the short game that had plagued me for years.

When James is at T.P.I. coaching one of his players, I make a point to watch "The Master" at work. James has an amazing amount of knowledge and a real gift for communicating his message. I'm constantly picking his brain to improve my understanding of how all the pieces fit together. If you struggle with your short game and think that you'll never get better, trust me: It's not your fault. You just need the right information. Information is the key to success. James Sieckmann has the correct information and experience to help you quickly build a short-game arsenal for maximum confidence from 120 yards and in. Once you understand the secrets to making solid contact with a wedge, there's no looking back. By understanding the fundamental differences between the full swing and the different types of wedge shots, you'll finally see why you've struggled for so long. Better yet, you'll be the envy of your regular foursome.

I hope you enjoy James's book. I know your short game will thank you forever!

DR. GREG ROSE
Cofounder, Titleist Performance Institute
Oceanside, Calif.
March 21, 2014

PREFACE

'm excited for you and the improvements you're about to make to your short game. I've played professional golf on the PGA and Champions tours for more than twenty-five years, and every week in event pro-ams I see firsthand the devastating wedge-play struggles of the recreational golfer. Sometimes I'll ask a pro-am partner why they do the things they do from 100 yards and in. I'm shocked at the answers and concerned at how bad the information is that they're carrying in their heads. I do my best to help them as we go, but I feel like an army of one battling thousands.

James Sieckmann is my personal short-game coach. In this book, he'll explain the true wedge fundamentals and how to fuse them into your game. I'm positive that as you work your way through the book, you'll clearly see why your short game is failing you. It's not your skill level; it's your information. The players I've tried to help haven't been given the tools to get the job done. But those days are over. I see a great, confident, and consistent short game in your future.

James and I have worked together for more than twenty years. In the early days, I was lucky enough to befriend and practice with the great Seve Ballesteros and see his short-game magic up close. James has studied Seve's techniques intensely. We're a perfect match in that we both believe that Ballesteros's wedge work is unmatched in the history of the game. In basing his systems on Seve's methods, James has become the best short-game instructor in the world.

My short game has improved to a point where I can confidently (and without feeling too boastful) say that it's right there at the top of the PGA and Champions tours. I owe it all to our hard work and James's ability to communicate and teach with passion.

Enjoy the read and the process.

TOM PERNICE JR.
Nashville, Tenn.
April 25, 2014

YOUR
SHORT GAME
SOLUTION

CHAPTER 1

THE DAWNING OF
A NEW WEDGE ERA

Most weekend players—and a surprisingly large number of Tour professionals—are working hard but failing to develop the simple short-game skills required to reach their true scoring potential. It's not their fault, because what most instructors have taught about the short game for decades is, in a word, wrong.

t's an exciting time in golf instruction. Old-school coaching—and its reliance on hunches and guesswork—is evolving into a modern, fact-based discipline. Credit goes to the massive and recent influx of science and scientific study in every area of the game, including the full swing, short game, putting, motor learning, and biomechanics. Many undeniable truths have been discovered, and just as many myths have been dispelled. Coaches are seeking and sharing knowledge based on research and testing instead of blindly accepting tradition, cutting the emotional ties that allow faulty theories to live beyond their time. We've come to that point in the short game. The earth is no longer flat.

This research revolution has been a long time coming. In 1994, when I first started teaching the methods that you'll read about in this book, they were often met with a sideways stare from the golf establishment. I swam upstream for years, but remained steadfast as I continued to learn and grow in my beliefs. It has taken more than two decades, but the tide has turned. A new generation of research-savvy coaches, as well as many of the old guard that once balked at my techniques, have come to embrace my Finesse and Distance Wedge Systems, which you'll become familiar with in this book as the "how to" short-game methods. Truth be told, I didn't invent these techniques—great players have used them since the dawn of the sand wedge. But they were closely guarded secrets known and shared by an elite few. I was just lucky enough to come across some of these individuals and, through four serendipitous events and a lot of hard work, systematically unlock them.

In *Your Short Game Solution*, I describe with simplicity and clarity what you need to do to make these methods your own and develop a world-class short game. In addition, I've created a practice plan for you to follow so that you'll not only make a quantum leap in performance, but sustain it over time. With just a little discipline and focus, you'll develop the confidence, swagger, and shot-making flair that all great short-game players share.

ORIGIN OF THE SYSTEM

To truly absorb what lies ahead, I think it's important to understand the roots of my beliefs. How did the shortcomings of a failed mini-tour player come to figure into *your* improvement plan? Why is discipline more important to succeeding than a huge investment in time? How did a little-known coach from a flyover state steadily become one of the most sought-after short-game experts in professional golf, with a client list that now includes more than eighty PGA and LPGA Tour players? The answers lie in the tangled history of my wedge systems, a must-read tale that will help ignite your quest for your lowest scores.

Part 1: Meet the Sieckmanns

I grew up in Omaha, Nebraska, as one of three sons in a golf-crazed family. My oldest brother, Tom, was nearly ten years my senior and played golf at Oklahoma State University. I was seven when he went off to college and not that much older when he left O.S.U. early to compete on the Asian and South American tours, beginning in 1977. Tom was sort of the "shining light" in our clan. His professional career would eventually span seventeen years, and he notched nine victories worldwide, including the 1988 Anheuser-Busch Golf Classic on the PGA Tour.

I was proud of Tom, and some of his skills must have rubbed off on me, because I shot 76 as a ten-year-old and won quite a few tournaments as a junior with minimal formal coaching. As such, I did what felt natural. I had very few swing thoughts and played with a lot of confidence. Golf was fun then—zero fear, all dreams. I parlayed my instincts into several good showings and an athletic scholarship to the University of Nebraska. As my journey in golf continued, Tom and I reconnected both as brothers and competitive golfers. There was a lot I could learn from him. Little did I know what was in store.

Part 2: Meet Seve Ballesteros

In addition to being a great golfer, Tom is smart and introspective. An avid reader of history with a keen mind for finance, he was anything but your typical pro athlete. Among other things, he taught himself Spanish. I'm sure it was more like "Spanglish," but that didn't stop him from speaking it during playing stints in South America and Europe. Serendipity struck for the first time when Tom's blind disregard for proper linguistics caught the ear of a young Spaniard at the 1977 Colombian Open in Medellín. Barely nineteen years old, Seve Ballesteros heard Tom's broken Spanish and felt comforted. After all, he was five thousand miles away from home and Spanish was the only language he knew.

"Seve and I just kind of hit it off," remembers Tom. "He appreciated that I was trying to speak Spanish and that I was interested in the short game. Even then he was already the best. The world just didn't know it yet." Ballesteros would forever cement his place in the public consciousness with his victory at the 1979 British Open at the age of twenty-two. By then, my brother and the young Spaniard were already good friends, working on their short games together and playing practice rounds whenever they could.

In 1984, Tom qualified for the U.S. Open at Winged Foot. I remember the phone call from him like it was yesterday: "Come meet me at the Open. You have to see Seve Ballesteros in person."

I was nineteen years old. It was my first trip to New York, my first time at a major, and I was inside the ropes, caddying no less. I felt a bit out of my league, so I kept my head down and focused on being the best caddy I could. Tom played nine holes by himself on Monday afternoon. On Tuesday, we paired up with two of his friends. One was Seve, who oozed confidence and competence. As the saying goes, men wanted to be him and women wanted to be with him—and you could tell that from a hundred yards away. The other friend was second-year pro Tom Pernice Jr., whom Tom had befriended on the Asian Tour. Like my brother, Pernice loved to practice short-game shots and hung around Seve every chance he could.

"When I first met Seve, he was only twenty years old and he's hitting shots like I've never seen," Pernice recalls today. "He hit softer shots with his 3-iron out of the bunker than we could with a sand wedge. During practice rounds, we'd put him in situations he had never seen and he'd pull off a ridiculous shot on the first attempt."

That day at Winged Foot, the two Toms played Seve and Wayne Grady in a $20 Nassau. "Tom and Tom have no chance," I thought, but they managed to win the total and several presses. Seve was not amused. After the round, I accompanied my brother into the players' locker room. We sat down to eat lunch and were joined a few minutes later by Seve. He was a gentleman and made a point to include me in the conversation, at one point lecturing me not to use "being young" as an excuse for failing. (I had missed the cut at the second stage of U.S. Open qualifying just two weeks earlier.) Needless to say, I became a Ballesteros fan for life on the spot.

My brother, Tom (second from right) playing his Tuesday practice round at the 1991 Masters with Seve Ballesteros (far right) and José María Olazábal (center). Tom's friendship with Seve lasted thirty-four years, and much of my Finesse and Distance Wedge Systems are based on my brother's and Ballesteros's techniques. (I'm in the caddy uniform, far left.)

Part 3: On My Own

I played well for the Cornhuskers in spurts, especially during my freshman and sophomore seasons, but it was obvious, even then, that I would need to improve my short game to realize my dreams. In hindsight, it was the beginning of the end. Why I didn't recognize or pay particular attention to what Seve and my brother were doing technique-wise at Winged Foot, and during several encounters thereafter, I'll never know. I had the best short-game player in history standing right in front of my face, and I learned nothing. Instead, I bought and read books and magazines, falling victim to the blind hunches, guesswork, and accepted myths of the teaching establishment:

> *A chip is just a miniature full swing.*
> *Keep your head still.*
> *Keep your lead arm straight and don't ever let the clubhead pass your hands.*

The tips looked good on paper, but they certainly didn't help. My response when they failed was to practice even harder and longer—surely the problem was with me and not the establishment. I was twenty years old and, suddenly, my growth as a golfer had flatlined. Even worse, I was studying myself out of my natural gifts.

Nevertheless, I followed in my brother's footsteps after graduating and set out to compete on the South American Tour. It was 1989; five years had passed since my lunch with Seve at Winged Foot. After competing in Brazil, Argentina, and Chile and failing to qualify for the 1990 PGA Tour season (my first of three Q-School busts), I flew to the Philippines for the first of eleven tournaments over the span of eleven weeks on the Asian Tour. I knew I was struggling, but I was confident that if I worked hard, something would eventually click and take my game to the next level. The click turned out to be a "clank." I *labored* in Asia for nearly three months. My poor performance around the greens persisted like a bad houseguest. At some point, I stopped feeling comfortable over the ball. Shots I had hit day in and day out since I was a little boy suddenly felt

foreign. I started to fear little shots, and as a golfer there's nothing worse than fear. So I did the only thing I knew how to do: work *harder*. While the rest of the players went sightseeing, I emptied shag bags hitting pitches and chips under the hot Asian sun. I practiced nonstop—no deviation, no routine, all technique.

Starting to feel it all go wrong at the 1989 Chile Open in Santiago.

Apparently, working hard on the wrong things the wrong way isn't much of a strategy. The doubts I had about my game increased with every missed cut and 50th-place finish. I'd replay poor chips and pitches in my head at night and wonder what was wrong with me. Despite my sincere efforts, I was getting worse, not better.

In hindsight, I had hit the perfect trifecta of failure: I was working with faulty information, I was training ineffectively, and I was a malicious self-critic. What I'd give to know then what I do now, but obviously that's not the way life works.

The life of a traveling Tour player can be a difficult one, especially when you're filling up passports in the process. Add in poor results and stretching every dollar so you can play the next event, and it's a life you don't want, dreams be damned. I hung in there for four years. In 1992, in a hotel room in New Delhi after posting yet another 50-something finish, I quit. Enough was enough. I was ready for a new chapter in my life. I flew home to Nebraska.

Part 4: The Pelz Experience

Not long after my plane hit the tarmac at Eppley Airfield in Omaha in the late spring of 1992, I proposed to my girlfriend, Michele Neal, and took a full-time coaching job at the Dave Pelz Short Game School in Austin, Texas. It was a reunion of sorts; my brother saw Dave a lot over the years, and I'd often tag along to Austin to watch them work, or go by myself to practice when it got too cold in Omaha. I knew Dave well, and was lucky and thankful that he thought enough of me to give me a new beginning.

I worked for a couple of years in Austin and another at the Pelz School in Boca Raton, Florida. I matured quickly as a coach, and I owe much of my growth to Dave. Although today we don't see eye to eye on a lot of things about the short game, he was the first person to challenge me to think critically about mechanics and to understand how people learn and train most effectively. He's a great coach and an outstanding person, and I owe him an awful lot.

Part 5: The Ponte Vedra Experience

I worked for Dave through March of 1994, until one of my closest friends and former sponsors, Steve Shanahan, established a partnership with my brother in the development of a new course in Omaha and asked me to direct the golf academy. Working for Pelz had been great, but this was too prime an opportunity to pass up: I'd get to be my own boss to some extent, teach my own methods, and raise a family in my hometown. Between farewells to Dave and the late-spring grand opening of my new academy at Shadow Ridge Country Club, I had two months of downtime. With nothing to do but go to the beach, I accepted an invitation to caddy for my brother at the Players Championship in Ponte Vedra Beach, Florida. Serendipity had struck again.

Given another chance to walk among the greatest players in the world, I wasn't going to waste it this time. I arrived at TPC Sawgrass in March of 1994 with Tom's bag on one shoulder and a video camera on the other. With a thirst for short-game knowledge, I filmed every great short-game player I could find. In addition to my brother, I saw Raymond Floyd and Corey Pavin, smoothly hitting chips onto a practice green. There was Greg Norman, working on his bunker technique—and making it look easy. On the range: Wayne Grady and Jodie Mudd dialing in wedge shots from every distance. And of course, Seve— *The Master*—doing everything. Tom played and practiced with Seve on Monday and Tuesday, and I recorded almost every short-game swing Seve made, probably to his chagrin. I can still recall him hitting practice shots out of the pot bunker behind the fourth green. He splashed five of the softest spinning bunker shots I had ever seen, all finishing within a yard or so of the pin. When he put his club in his bag, I about fell over when I saw that it was a 56-degree sand wedge and not a lob wedge. Once again, he had made the near impossible seem mundane.

Tom finished the tournament twenty-four shots behind Greg Norman, who won the event by four over Fuzzy Zoeller. It wasn't a great week for my brother, but it was the start of something special for me. Even after teaching the short game for three years, I didn't feel like I really understood what great wedge play was all about, but my varied experiences had given me some insight on what questions to ask. Plus, I knew I had some one-of-a-kind material to study. As soon as my wife and I moved into our new apartment, I watched the videos. I decided that the best place to start was to wipe the slate clean, assume nothing, and simply catalog what great players did in every phase of the short game. After doing this for several weeks—dry-erase-marker lines all over the TV—some swing commonalities became apparent. After several more weeks, I could see how those commonalities were fitting together. "If this is what the best players in the world do," I thought, "then this is what I'm going to teach, regardless of what others think."

The videos both surprised and sickened me. They proved to me that everything I had ever been taught about short shots around the green—and practiced to exhaustion—was wrong. Things like "lean your weight toward the target at address," "keep your head still," and "don't break down or let the club pass your hands." I had hours of film showing the most talented wedge players on earth making these "mistakes" over and over. That was only the beginning; I drew plane lines, measured rhythm, and tried to quantify everything I could about both club and body movement. After a month, I pared what I saw on screen down to five big-ticket items and developed a way to understand how they fit together: my Finesse Wedge System (the Distance Wedge System came later). I have refined it every year since and believe in it more deeply with every coaching experience.

A frame-by-frame analysis of the wedge swings of Seve Ballesteros and other elite players proved beyond a doubt that what's often taught about the short game is wrong. For me, the secrets were on my TV screen.

Part 6: The Finesse Wedge System on Tour

For the next three years, I taught my system exclusively to the members at Shadow Ridge C.C. I didn't publish my findings or speak about them with other teaching professionals. Serendipity struck a third time via a phone call from Tom Pernice Jr. in 1996. (In addition to being one of my brother's best friends, "TP" and I played together in Asia and had also developed a friendship.) TP was playing the Hogan Tour that year (now the Web.com Tour) and was driving from an event in Wichita to another in Sioux City, Iowa, taking I-80 straight through Omaha. He was struggling mightily with his putting and, knowing I had worked for Dave Pelz, asked if I would take a look at him. I remember him misaligning his putter drastically on a straight-in six-footer at the start of the lesson, but as talented and hardworking as he was, it didn't take long to get him back on track. He called a month later and asked if I'd come to the Tour stop in Boise, Idaho, for another session. It was an interesting proposition, and I wanted to do it, but the numbers didn't add up. It would cost more in airfare, lodging, and three days of lost lessons at Shadow Ridge than what TP could pay me. I eventually agreed, but I asked him if he could find me some other players to work with in order to offset my expenses. Thankfully, a few other players said yes. One of them was Charlie Wi, a recent graduate of UC Berkeley who was playing in his first year as a professional. Just like that, my life as a Tour instructor had begun. I've coached Tom and Charlie continually since 1996. Their loyalty to me has been immeasurable, and it has been a symbiotic relationship, for sure. Tour players ask tough questions, and they're so skilled that if you tell them the right things, they improve immediately. On the flip side, there's no faking it and nowhere to hide if you get it wrong. Coaching on Tour has taught me to think things all the way through, to be detail-oriented, prepared, and certain. I love the challenge it presents, and while I have many pro clients now, TP has been the difference maker. He studied and practiced with Seve for years, so he was already doing much of what I taught, and his enthusiasm and knowledge of the short game is unmatched by any player I've ever met. There's no doubt that I have learned more from him over the years than he has from me. As such, traveling has become a paradox; I don't particularly care for all of the hassles, and I hate being away from my family (I'm on the road about 150 days a year), but it's essential to my continued growth. Every time I leave my little patch of grass at Shadow Ridge to work on Tour, I pick up something new that helps me get better at my craft. Unfortunately, I have learned to love packing my suitcase.

Part 7: Soaring with Science

Despite working with an amazing client list, I toiled in relative anonymity my first thirteen years as a Tour coach, but I was satisfied with my career. Between my Academy at Shadow Ridge and raising two children with my wife, my plate seemed full but things were about to change. I don't know how many times serendipity can strike the middle of Nebraska, but it happened for a fourth time on my journey as a coach by way of an unexpected phone call from Dr. Greg Rose, co-founder of the Titleist Performance Institute (T.P.I.). Dr. Rose asked if I would be willing to work with PGA Tour player and Titleist staffer Ben Crane on his wedge game. I knew both Ben and Greg by reputation, but I had never spoken with either. We met a week later at the Madison Club in La Quinta,

California. I started the session like I do with any serious student by providing them with a copy of my *Short Game Notebook,* a manual detailing all of my beliefs and concepts. (As a former player, I know there's zero room for doubt or miscommunication when you're competing for a paycheck, and the *Notebook* leaves nothing to chance.) We worked for two days straight and got along beautifully. More important, Crane's wedge game improved. We worked again three weeks later at T.P.I., the day before the first round of the 2010 Farmers Insurance Open at Torrey Pines. Crane won—his first PGA Tour victory in almost five years—and led the field in scrambling at 89 percent. (The average scrambling percentage on Tour is around 57 percent.)

I took it that Dr. Rose was impressed, because he delivered several other Titleist staff players to me over the ensuing weeks. First Charley Hoffman and Brad Faxon, then Tom Purtzer and LPGA Tour player I.K. Kim. Eventually, I had to ask: "Why me?"

The answer, according to Dr. Rose, was a small paragraph I had written in my *Notebook* describing the correct sequence of events for a finesse wedge shot and what problems are created if you get it wrong.

Dr. Rose and T.P.I. co-founder Dave Phillips had already helped crack the kinematic sequence in full swings (the golf motion that proves the hips reach maximum speed first on the downswing, followed sequentially by the torso, arms, and finally, the clubhead). For many years, T.P.I. measured every Titleist golfer on both power swings and short-game swings, such as a 10-yard chip. By 2009, it had hundreds of Tour players in the system and had the full swing nailed. The problem? The data from the 3-D motion-capture system the company used to measure wedge swings didn't match up with the data generated on power swings. "With the short swing, we were still unsure about what the data was showing," says Rose.

That's because in a world-class finesse wedge swing, as I wrote in the *Notebook,* it's absolutely essential that the club starts down before the hips rotate, which is the reverse kinematic sequence of a power swing. Without the correct sequence, it's impossible to use the club correctly or to produce consistently solid contact (more on this in Chapter 4). My paragraph describing what great wedge players such as Seve Ballesteros do and why they do it matched Dr. Rose's scientific data to a T.

"James knew it," says Rose. "He knew it almost twenty years ago, before the term 'kinematic sequence' and 3-D motion capture were even around."

Dr. Rose and I ultimately helped each other. He got the answer to his short-game data problem, and by independently validating through science what I had carefully observed analyzing hours of video, he helped me gain notoriety as one of the premier short-game experts in the world. Over the years, I've shared these findings and other insights with more than 80 PGA and LPGA Tour players. Now, it's time to share these findings with you. The mistakes I made and the failures I endured as a golfer aren't limited to those who play for money. I see them everywhere and at every skill level. No other part of the game is littered with as many misconceptions—or is more poorly taught—than wedge play. That's why I'm excited that you've purchased *Your Short Game Solution*. The revolution is nearly over. Science has won, but it's time to get the message out. Let your journey begin!

CHAPTER 2

PERFORMANCE PITFALLS (OR WHY EVEN HARDWORKING, TALENTED PLAYERS OFTEN FAIL TO IMPROVE)

In most endeavors hard work pays off, but in golf it is very possible to work your way into higher scores and poor performance. Almost every course is rife with talented, dedicated players slaving away with great hope only to suffer this cruel irony.

I n this book we're going to dive into the techniques used by the best wedge players in the world inside 120 yards. However, if you invest time into making this quantum leap, it won't be good enough to just see that magic once in a while. You'll want to do it often and sustain your improvement over a long period of time.

In a perfect world, if you had natural talent and worked hard, you would improve. If you were a 10-handicap last year, you would be an 8-handicap today, and a 5-handicap next year. With each shot, you would gain experience, develop motor skill, and improve your feel. You'd experience constant growth, at least to the point where you maximized your athletic ability, and then maintain that level of play until there was a physical reason not to. Unfortunately, it's not a perfect world, and my lesson planner is full of players frustrated by the fact that, despite their best efforts and intentions, their game is in decline. I hear it all the time: "I've lost it," "I putt worse now than I did ten years ago," or "I have the yips." If this sounds familiar, you have my empathy. I've been there.

The sad thing is that this type of deterioration has nothing to do with getting older or breaking down physically. Rather, it's the result of something far more sinister: self-sabotage. That's right, WE are often the problem. Allow me to save you time and spare you potentially years of frustration by exposing the three most common performance pitfalls that victimize golfers, and more importantly, what to do about them.

PERFORMANCE PITFALLS

No. 1: Failing to Understand and/or Believe in Your Method

You have to understand what you're doing and why you're doing it. Your fundamentals must blend together to create a system that's clearly defined and rarely changed. You also need to trust that if you execute, your swing will produce success. Without this understanding and commitment, your intuitive human response to poor shots will become destructive. You'll tinker. You'll think too much. You'll try anything, hoping by some miracle to find the "secret" to greatness.

The bad news is that no matter who you are, bad shots are coming. It's golf, and we aren't robots. Golf by nature is fickle, and the line between good and bad is very small. Ben Hogan once said that he knew he would hit six perfect shots and six terrible shots every round, and that his score was largely determined by those in between. Do you think Mr. Hogan threw his system in the waste bin and moved on to the next thing after a few bad shots or rounds, or did he set his plan and then work until he mastered it? Would your answer differ if I told you that the time it takes to master something starts over every time you make a change? Of course it would. Changes can be good, but only if you think them through and are positive that they fit within the context of your overall

Hard at work with Ben Crane and his caddy, Joel Stock, at the 2014 Honda Classic. Great wedge players practice with a purpose, and they don't make a change unless it's clearly thought out and fits with the other fundamentals in their swing and setup.

plan. If not, you're bound to fall back. Looking for the "secret" is a near-sided response of the insecure and undisciplined.

This reminds me of an experience I had caddying for my brother while I was still a student at the University of Nebraska. I can't recall the exact year (it was sometime in the mid-1980s), but Tom was entered in the Tucson Open at TPC Star Pass (now Starr Pass Golf Club). He was hitting chip shots onto the practice green when his buddy and fellow competitor, Gary Hallberg, called Tom over to watch him hit a few putts, stating in a joyous voice that he had just discovered "the secret to putting." Tom and I ambled over and watched Hallberg hole three 20-footers in a row. He turned back to us, and with a big smile, shared his epiphany. After a brief full-swing warm-up, Tom and Gary went out to the 10th tee, caddies in tow, to play their practice round. On the tenth green, Hallberg seemed frozen as he stood over his birdie putt. I thought he was doing his best Jack Nicklaus impersonation, but after a good half-minute he rose up out of his putting posture. He wasn't smiling this time. Instead, he was visibly embarrassed and said, "Hey, Tom—what did I say the secret to putting was again?"

Having so many secrets that you can't remember them doesn't lead to long-term success. "Berger" is a great guy and supremely talented, but please don't make the same mistake that he did. Secrets and quick fixes may work for the day or even a week, but a bad round is surely coming. That's the way golf is. Then what? More tinkering and a desperate search for the next magic bullet: a new grip, an open stance—anything. Don't be that guy! That guy is one more bad round away from being *completely* lost, with four different swings and a closet full of clubs that "don't work."

No. 2: Training Ineffectively

In today's busy world, time is precious, so it's critical that you structure your range sessions for maximum effectiveness. This seems obvious, but an overwhelming majority of weekend players don't know how to practice to stay on track and develop their skills. They go to the range without a real plan, remain in their comfort zone and mindlessly hit shot after shot from a pile until they become tired, bored, or run out of time. Sure, they'll make a small adjustment here and there as they react to their shots, but they won't produce substantive changes. And they'll keep doing it again and again. Surely this isn't what effective training looks like.

One of the keys to growth is a willingness to be uncomfortable. I've often had a student tell me after a lesson, "I can't believe how awkward that was at the beginning, but how well it worked and how good it felt as the lesson progressed."

My usual reply is "that's why self-coaching seldom works." Be honest: When you practice on your own, do you try things that make you that uncomfortable, or commit to changes long enough to make them feel natural? Great players are willing to do whatever is required to be great, regardless of how strange or awkward it feels.

Case in point: I was recently in San Diego to work with LPGA Tour player I.K. Kim on her short game. I met I.K. at the range as she was hitting balls and asked if she was ready to start her lesson. She said she needed just a bit more time to complete her "speed sets." I stepped aside as her caddy spread a towel on the ground and I.K. proceeded to perform the drill (ten swings with a heavy driver followed by ten with a light one) from her knees. She said the speed sets were designed to increase the rotational speed of her upper-body. She ripped one after the other 200 yards-plus in the air.

Impressed, I asked her if she was ready to go. "Not quite yet," she responded, "I need to hit ten left-handed 5-irons first." She topped, sliced, and chunked her way through all ten. This drill helped her stretch and strengthen the muscles opposite the ones she normally works, which reduces imbalances and helps prevent injury. "Now I'm ready," she said, and off we went to the short-game area. She wasn't worried about what others on the range were thinking. She wasn't worried about feeling awkward. She was completely focused on what she was trying to accomplish and more than willing to be uncomfortable during the process.

I.K. Kim performing her specialized "speed sets" to increase upper-body rotational speed. It's worth repeating: Great players are willing to do whatever it takes to improve performance.

Throughout this book, I'll define the fundamentals and the essential skills needed to perform at a high level. Growth demands that you have effective ways to work on both of them. You'll be asked to try some things that may cause some stares and/or get you out of your comfort zone. Embrace them. They're the keys to turning your range sessions into learning sessions.

No. 3: Thinking like a Chump, Instead of a Champ

Another reason that hardworking, talented players often fail to improve is that they lack the mental-performance skills necessary to play at or near their athletic potential, especially in difficult environments. This isn't an earth-shattering revelation. A player's mental state and attributes (i.e., concentration, resiliency, toughness, and confidence) obviously affect performance, but how do you improve these things? Can you exude confidence before good results or only after? What exactly is mental performance—is it physical, emotional, or both? And if it's a crucial piece of the performance pie, should you just leave it to chance and hope you find it, or should you work on improving it every day? In regard to the last question, the answer is an emphatic "yes," which means that my new question for you is: "When you went to the practice facility today, did you work on improving your mental skills?"

I'm not an academic and have no real formal training in psychology, but I experienced as a player the patterns and behaviors that I now know to be destructive, and as a Tour coach, I've witnessed the mental habits of some of the best players in the world. Through these experiences, I've learned to recognize what clearly does and doesn't work at both the pro and amateur level, and I'm confident that as you progress through this book, you'll see the error of your ways and get pointed in the right direction.

OTHER PITFALLS FOR THOUGHT

There's one more common performance pitfall that's more pertinent to your power game, but it's still an issue of major concern for your short game: a failure to optimize your equipment. No, not your clubs, set makeup, lie and bounce angles, grinds, etc. (which are important items that I'll touch on in later chapters). My bigger concern is the other piece of equipment that you bring to the course every day: your body. Weakness and outright physical limitations hinder many players from executing fundamentals. I do my best to account for this when I start working with a new student. I have assessment procedures and make subtle adaptations for each student in their technical plan based on what their bodies can and can't do. Plain and simple, your body's functionality is a critical piece of the performance puzzle. You can't neglect it.

Honestly, biomechanics are a little beyond my scope of expertise, but it's easy to find information and people who know how to help. My advice: visit mytpi.com and peruse the site's strength and mobility videos. It's all cutting-edge stuff designed purely for golfers. Also, consider having a strength-and-conditioning expert assess you and prescribe a personalized, golf-specific fitness plan.

CHAPTER 3

A PLAN FOR SHORT-GAME SUCCESS

The person with the best and most-accurate information has a huge advantage. There's no place in short-game mastery for emotional judgments or ego.

My wedge systems are more than a random collection of swing moves, positions, and feels. They're a carefully orchestrated plan that allows you to improve skills that, when combined, automatically produce the swing(s) you need to handle any shot within 120 yards of the pin. As such, it's critical that you know where you are within the construct of the system every step of the way. In order to effectively stay on course, you'll need to reallocate two very important resources in your daily life: time and money.

Time: Dedicate 15 minutes per day for planning and practicing the mental-performance tips outlined in Chapter 8. Anyone can manage an extra 15 minutes of free time per day, and let's be honest—if I.K. Kim is willing to do speed sets off her knees in front of dozens of onlookers, you can certainly spend 15 minutes over your morning coffee to ponder your short game.

Money: Don't worry—my systems are going to *save* you money, not drain your checking account. With my plan, there's no need to waste precious dollars on quick fixes. Your only outlay is a few bucks on a quality notebook, which you'll use as a journal to map out your plan and chart your progress. Title it "My Short Game Solution" or anything else that motivates you. On the inside cover, write a realistic six-month performance goal, such as "By next summer, I'll shoot in the 70s for at least half of my rounds." Make it something that'll get you excited about practicing and mastering the techniques in this book. Divide your journal into four equal sections with the following headings: 1) Finesse Wedges, 2) Greenside Bunkers, 3) Distance Wedges, and 4) Working My Plan.

The act of writing heightens your commitment and makes it more difficult to stray from the plan. As my father, Whitey, once told me, "A dull pencil is sharper than a sharp mind."

Of course, I'll guide you each step of the way. As we progress through this book (and your journal), you'll learn the key elements in each section, including simple setup and swing concepts for optimal technique, a comprehensive training plan, and championship thinking habits. You'll be working smarter and more effectively than 99 percent of the golfers you know while avoiding common roadblocks to sustainable growth.

STEP 1: REBOOT YOUR COMPUTER

Wipe your mental slate clean and forget what you *think* you know about the short game, just as I did when I sat down to analyze the videos I shot at the 1994 Players Championship. Having a clear mind from this point forward is critical, because it's certain that most of what you learned about the short game in the past is wrong. Also, choose whom you listen to carefully as you progress through your journal, because there's a ton of bad information out there, especially from instructors who should know better. Golf is a tradition-rich game riddled with concepts—often passed down from generation to generation—that just don't pass muster when looked at objectively using a modern-day, scientific approach. I'll expose these myths for what they really are throughout this book, but let's look at one of them in-depth right now, so you can learn the inherent disadvantages of using bad information and how emotion (and your ego) can cloud judgment.

Myth: Lay up to a Full-Swing Yardage

As I mentioned in Chapter 1, I became the short-game coach for Ben Crane and Charley Hoffman just prior to the start of the 2010 PGA Tour season. By the end of the year, Crane had won twice (the Farmers Insurance Open and CIMB Asia Pacific Classic) and Charley once (the Deutsche Bank Championship, with a sizzling, final-round 62). One of the things I do at the conclusion of any year is to schedule a team meeting with each of my clients to take inventory of what we've done well (I assess both my and the client's performance) and figure out what we can do better going forward. Usually, I do a lot of statistical research in preparation for each team meeting, and in the case with Crane in the fall of 2010, I found myself paying particular attention to how Tour pros execute lay-up shots. It was obvious that the majority of them were listening to old-school instruction that said it was better to lay up to a yardage that allows you to make a full swing on the following shot. However, independent studies show that it's better to push the ball up as close to the green as possible, and that the closer you are to the pin, the closer you'll end up to the hole after the next shot.

Of course, there are some important qualifiers to these research conclusions. First, the sample size needs to be big enough to get an accurate picture of what's really going on. Second, being in the fairway matters—if you're forced to play the shot following your lay-up from the rough, you can add approximately nine feet in distance from the pin compared with a similar shot hit from the fairway. Third, there are occasional situations (such as downwind shots to front pins) when laying up to a full-swing distance (so you can create extra spin) is prudent. Lastly, knocking the ball as close as possible to the green on a lay-up shot only works if you're adept from shorter distances (which you soon will be). Nevertheless, given the opportunity to push the ball up to a spot that's 50 yards from the green or to lay back to 110 yards, the numbers clearly show that laying up closer is the better choice.

After presenting this data to Crane and his caddy, Joel Stock, at the team meeting, they immediately changed their approach and Crane started making more birdies. The proof is in Crane's improved performance on par 5s (the holes most likely to require a lay-up) between 2010 and 2012.

Ben Crane: Par-5 Birdie or Better Percentage

Season	Birdie Percentage	PGA Tour Rank
2010	41.1%	77th
2012	48.4%	13th

Statistics courtesy PGATour.com

I had a tougher time convincing Charley Hoffman when I presented the data to him in our 2011 team meeting. He admitted that he *always* left 110 yards to the pin on a lay-up, because he was comfortable from that distance and that he "sucked" from 50 yards. We looked at his PGA Tour ShotLink data. He was right—he landed shots hit from 100 to 125 yards an average of 17' 5" from the pin in 2010, good enough for 11th place on Tour in that stat category. He was also right in that he wasn't very good from the 50- to 75-yard range—he actually ranked 119th. The kicker, however, is that his average proximity to the pin from 50 to 75 yards was 16' 3", more than a foot closer than shots hit from his comfort zone! This is a great example of how ego and emotion can affect judgment, but you can't blame Charley. Imagine how good the ball looks in the air and the confidence you feel when you stop a shot 17 feet from the pin from 110 yards, and how you'd beat yourself up by landing a much shorter shot just one foot closer. But the reality is that you've left yourself a 6 percent shorter putt! Numbers don't lie. Emotions do.

Convinced by this data, Charley recommitted himself to both laying up closer to the green and improving his performance from 50 to 75 yards—the bugaboo distance that convention had forced him to not only avoid on the course, but to scratch from his practice routine. Now he works on it daily. Did removing emotion from his game and bucking old-school advice work? The numbers below tell the story.

Charley Hoffman

Season ·	Proximity to Pin from 50–75 Yards (Rank)	Scoring Average (Rank)
2011	16' 3" (119th)	71.09 (122nd)
2013	11' 6" (11th)	70.50 (43rd)

Statistics courtesy PGATour.com

Working with Charley Hoffman at the 2013 Arnold Palmer Invitational on shots from 30 to 70 yards. Emotions and bad information had led him to avoid this distance range despite statistical evidence that mastering it would lead to lower scores.

If bad decisions are a problem for Tour players, imagine the mistakes that *you're* making. The double whammy is that yours are more difficult to determine. When I'm working with a Tour pro, I have a ton of statistical information at my disposal, so not only can we see what needs improving, we can check the numbers to determine if he or she is making any progress. When an amateur shows up for a lesson, I have nothing to go on except their opinion. Clearly, this isn't optimal. Frustrated by this fact, my brother Tom and I started a golf statistics analysis site a few years back (golfimprovementplan.com). It allows my amateur students to record actual performance data from every round they play so I can assess their games using cold, hard facts, just like I do using PGA Tour ShotLink data with one of my pro clients.

The system works. Case in point: Doug, one of my regular students at Shadow Ridge, is a successful businessman, a 4-handicap and basically every-

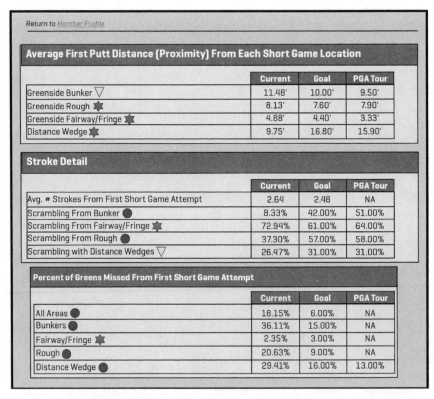

Return to Member Profile

Average First Putt Distance (Proximity) From Each Short Game Location

	Current	Goal	PGA Tour
Greenside Bunker ▽	11.48'	10.00'	9.50'
Greenside Rough ✸	8.13'	7.60'	7.90'
Greenside Fairway/Fringe ✸	4.88'	4.40'	3.33'
Distance Wedge ✸	9.75'	16.80'	15.90'

Stroke Detail

	Current	Goal	PGA Tour
Avg. # Strokes From First Short Game Attempt	2.64	2.48	NA
Scrambling From Bunker ●	8.33%	42.00%	51.00%
Scrambling From Fairway/Fringe ✸	72.94%	61.00%	64.00%
Scrambling From Rough ●	37.30%	57.00%	58.00%
Scrambling with Distance Wedges ▽	26.47%	31.00%	31.00%

Percent of Greens Missed From First Short Game Attempt

	Current	Goal	PGA Tour
All Areas ●	18.15%	6.00%	NA
Bunkers ●	36.11%	15.00%	NA
Fairway/Fringe ✸	2.35%	3.00%	NA
Rough ●	20.63%	9.00%	NA
Distance Wedge ●	29.41%	16.00%	13.00%

A screenshot from a student's statistical profile on golfimprovementplan.com easily shows where the most work is needed. Looking at hard data is the only reliable way to judge where you are in your plan and where you need to focus your efforts to improve.

thing a coach hopes for in a student. He's in great physical shape, skillful, and disciplined, and he burns with an intense desire to improve. He showed up for his monthly lesson one afternoon and asked if we could work on his driving. "I need to drive it 10 yards farther so I can hit more par 5s in two," he said. He was certain this would save him a minimum of two shots per round. I was less than convinced, so we went into my office to check his data on golfimprovementplan.com, which told a completely different tale. His distance numbers suggested that he was already driving the ball at a scratch-handicap level, so that wasn't where the extra four strokes were coming from. We moved on to his bunker play, and discovered that he was failing to get the ball on the green on more than a third of his attempts, and needed four shots to get up and down more than 25 percent of the time. Moreover, his lag putts from 30 to 60 feet were getting no closer than nine feet to the hole, which resulted in two three-putts per round. We skipped the driving and went straight to the practice bunker and then the putting green. Within weeks, he had reached his goal.

Doug is just one example of how even a normal amount of ego and bad information can stop a player from recognizing the weak areas in his or her game. Everyone wants to drive the ball 10 yards farther, including me, but at what cost? Certainly not at neglecting key areas of the short game that, in Doug's case, added up to four extra shots per round.

PGA Tour Confidential: Ben Crane

"I check my statistics regularly, and consult the members of my team and set my practice plan accordingly. I don't chase results daily, but I keep a long-term view and know that if my fundamentals are good and I'm doing the right things, the results will take care of themselves."

STEP 2: OPTIMIZE YOUR WEDGES

You'll get the most out of the Finesse and Distance Wedge Systems if your wedges are right not only for you, but also for the conditions in which you typically play. Obviously, everyone's ideal set needs to be personalized, and since I don't know what's currently in your bag, the best I can do is offer up what I think are the most important factors when selecting the right mix of wedges. Hopefully, this will answer many of the questions you have about wedge design and performance, but if not, your local PGA professional can. Just a little time spent with a knowledgeable fitter experimenting with different lofts, bounce angles, and grinds—and seeing how these specifications affect contact, ball flight, and turf interaction—will go a long way toward maximizing your improvement.

Answers to Common Wedge Questions

How many wedges should I carry? The correct answer depends on how far you typically hit the ball. If you're a power player (i.e., you can hit your pitching wedge 130 yards or farther), you should carry four wedges: Consider a loft combination of 46, 50, 55, and 60 degrees. This will likely give you two wedge options for shots less than 100 yards with no more than a 20-yard gap between successive clubs (an accepted "golden rule" for set makeups). If you're a short hitter (shots hit with your pitching wedge carry 100 yards or less), you can get away with just two wedges (a 48-degree pitching wedge and a 56-degree sand wedge, for example). If, like most recreational players, you fall somewhere in the middle, you should opt for a three-wedge setup, again paying mind to the golden rule. Consider a 48-degree pitching wedge, a 54-degree sand wedge, and a 60-degree lob wedge.

It's interesting to note that after the USGA banned the use of box (or square) grooves in 2009, many Tour players ditched their 60-degree lob wedges for 58-degree models, because the new wedges (which featured legal and lower-spinning "V" grooves) launched the ball too high. Grooves have improved since that time, and lofts are trending back to pre-2009 levels, but players with better technique generally require less loft. And before you ask, there's never a need to carry a wedge with more than 60 degrees of loft, especially after learning and mastering my system.

What bounce options should I use? The bounce on a wedge is the angle formed between the leading edge of the club and the high point of the sole (usually the trailing edge). Most manufacturers indicate the bounce angle with a stamp on the club itself. For example, my Titleist Vokey sand wedge is stamped with a "54.11," which means it has 54 degrees of loft and 11 degrees of bounce. In general, more bounce is better in soft conditions and for players who tend to dig into the turf, while less bounce is better in firm conditions and for players who tend to "pick" the ball and generate a higher ball flight. Again, these are just generalities. The smart thing to do is to cover the bases with, say, a sand wedge with a lot of bounce (11 to 14 degrees) and a lob wedge with less (4 to 7 degrees). That way, you'll always have a wedge with the ideal amount of bounce for the situation at hand. (We'll delve into this much more deeply as the book progresses.)

What about the shaft, lie angle, and grinds? I'm a big fan of using the same type of shaft in your wedges as you do in your irons, if only to maintain the same feel throughout your set. Specialty wedge shafts manufactured to add spin provide marginal benefit for most recreational players. The lie angle on your wedges (the angle formed by the shaft and the ground when the club sits at address), on the other hand, makes a huge difference, especially with your most-lofted wedge. Ninety percent of the shots you'll hit with this club take place within 20 yards of the pin, and if we did a lie-angle test for these situations, we'd find that the optimal lie angle is much flatter than what's needed on full-swing shots. My irons are all 1-degree upright, but my lob wedge is 1-degree flat. Whatever you do, make sure the lie angles on your wedges don't cause the heel section to dig into the turf through impact. I prefer the L, M, and T grinds on the Titleist Vokey SM5 wedge because they create extra relief in the heel and trailing edge and provide greater versatility than standard grinds. But, again, your local PGA professional can help make sure that the lie angles of your wedges are a match for your game.

The grind on your wedges (the general look and shape of the sole) also matters. I recommend more relief (or "grind") in the heel and trailing edge. This allows you to open the clubface at address to play higher shots off tight lies without adding too much effective bounce. In addition, the extra relief pushes the bounce angle toward the leading edge, which will benefit you when you set the clubface square at address. This extra versatility makes it easier to hit successful shots from a variety of ground conditions and lies.

Short-Game Mastery

Momentum is a cruel mistress. You can't afford to take significant steps backward on your journey. Your new advantage is that you're going to follow a plan that's Tour-proven. Most importantly, you'll be working hard and smart, avoiding the common pitfalls that derail even the most talented, well-meaning players. When you turn this page you'll dive headfirst into the mechanics of the Finesse Wedge System and start formulating your plan (remember to buy that journal!). Because of what you've already learned in the first three chapters of this book, the process will be logical and simple to follow without requiring massive amounts of time. All you'll need is focus and a little discipline. I know from experience the value in having a plan you believe in, and then following it to its completion. It allows you to get more out of your practice and enjoy your game more, because you'll no longer be chasing short-term outcomes and riding a roller coaster of emotions. Instead, you'll be chasing the short game of your dreams.

CHAPTER 4

FINESSE WEDGES: TOUR TECHNIQUES FOR ANY PLAYER

As your goals change from generating power to creating finesse, the way you use the club also changes, and therefore, so does your technique.

One of the first things I noticed while digesting the videotape from the 1994 Players Championship was that the pros' setup and swing characteristics on short shots looked very different from their full-power swings. As I began to note all the differences, a thought struck me: Why would one setup and swing be the same when the goals for each type of shot are so dramatically different?

Goals: Power Swings vs. Finesse Swings

POWER	FINESSE
Maximize clubhead speed	Control clubhead speed
Create a penetrating ball flight	Create a soft ball flight
Decrease loft at impact (with an iron)	Use the loft and bounce of the club at impact
Take a divot in front of the ball (with an iron)	Brush the turf

This revelation immediately cemented itself as the foundation for my Finesse Wedge System. In fact, understanding what's optimal for power and what's critical for finesse—and realizing that they diametrically oppose each other—is the first step toward attaining wedge greatness.

If there's just one skill in wedge play that trumps all others, it's a player's ability to make great contact. There are two types of contact, however: 1) ball/club; and 2) club/ground. In the finesse game, you want to optimize and be consistent with both. Without this ability, your focus, creativity, and confidence will ultimately suffer, and distance control becomes next to impossible. To master your ability to produce solid contact, you'll need to absorb and practice the following five fundamentals. These are the non-negotiable pillars of my Finesse Wedge System. Your short-game lesson starts now.

FINESSE WEDGE FUNDAMENTAL NO. 1: SET UP FOR FINESSE

If the goal on short wedge shots is finesse rather than power, and you want to optimize both contact and control, what's the best setup to attain it? Check the photos below. This address position (for a standard 10-yard wedge shot) is 100 percent engineered for finesse, because it establishes the low point of the swing arc in front of the ball without jeopardizing the way the club is meant to perform. As the first "domino," so to speak, it is critical that we get this right. Let's go through all the setup elements, starting at the bottom and working our way up.

The finesse wedge setup.

STANCE: Set up with your feet evenly balanced and close together, with no more than four or five inches separating your heels. Keep your back foot square to the target line, but pull your front foot back a few inches and flare it out toward the target. This "flared" lead-foot position will aid your balance in the finish and allow your shoulders to remain relatively level as they rotate through the ball, both of which are necessary for great finesse wedge play.

BALL POSITION: On a standard-trajectory shot, play the ball a few inches inside your back foot. You've gotten it right if, after soling your wedge on the ground with your arms hanging down just forward of center, the shaft leans 3 to 7 degrees toward the target. You're probably leaning the shaft forward already, but only because you've made the mistake of straightening your lead arm, which creates both tension and shoulder tilt. Neither is good for consistent contact or a soft touch.

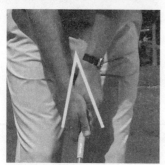

GRIP: Your trail-hand grip should be in your fingers and in a "weak" position on top of the club, similar to a standard putting grip. I call this a "Finesse Grip," and yes, you should have a different grip for your wedge play around the greens than you do off the tee. Check that the V formed by the thumb and forefinger of your trail hand points straight up at your sternum.

ARMS: It should feel like your arms are dangling softly from your shoulders—so softly that a slight bend remains in your lead elbow. It's also critical that there's "extension" or a small cup near the top of your lead wrist (wrinkles are a good sign). The cup is evidence that your ball position, grip, and arm hang are correct. Having and maintaining this cup in the lead wrist is key to making a correct backswing.

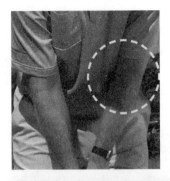

SHOULDERS: Your finesse grip, along with the correct arm hang, should set your shoulders fairly level with the ground. Setting up behind the ball with the kind of shoulder tilt you would use with your driver is a huge red flag and will severely limit your performance.

CHEST: Much like your stance, your chest should also be slightly rotated open to the target. Setting up in this manner not only moves the low point of your swing arc forward and in front of the ball, it also helps you rotate the toe of the club skyward in your backswing, which optimizes the way the club interacts with the turf through impact. Picture a flashlight attached to the middle of your sternum, and try to shine its light on the ground a few inches in front of the ball.

HEAD: From a face-on vantage point, your head should sit squarely over the middle of your sternum, which in turn should sit directly above your belt buckle. If done correctly, you should be able to trace a straight line from your nose through your zipper and the center of the space between your ankles. I call this being "stacked up" at address, which creates an evenly balanced stance.

Study these pictures and note what each feature looks like and, when you practice, what each feature *feels* like. It shouldn't take you long to get them all right. My suggestion? Practice setting up in front of a full-length mirror, focusing on one setup element at a time and using these photos as a reference. Start with a face-on view (with the mirror directly in front of you), and then finish with a down-the-line view (with the mirror off to your immediate right if you're a right-handed player, and to your immediate left if you're left-handed). From the down-the-line perspective, check that your weight is over the balls of your feet, your knees are "tall," with just a minimum amount of flex, and that you have enough hip hinge so that your arms hang directly down from your shoulders.

From a down-the-line perspective, check that your weight is over the balls of your feet, your legs are tall with just a minimum amount of flex, and that both your chest and the line formed by the top of your forearms are aligned similarly to your feet (open).

Don't be satisfied with nailing *some* of these setup fundamentals. You need them all. Each of them plays an essential role in the fundamentals to come and the overall functionality of both the club and your swing.

FINESSE WEDGE FUNDAMENTAL NO. 2:
SWING ON PLANE AND WITH AN OPEN CLUBFACE

Swinging the club on plane—that is, on a circle tilted the same number of degrees as the lie angle of your wedge (just imagine a circle resting on top of the shaft)—is the single most effective way to deliver the club for both finesse and control. The clubhead and your hands must both travel on this circle during your backswing *and* as you deliver the club into impact. Swinging on plane like this, minus any egregious errors, produces the ideal angle of attack for pure contact.

To show you what an on-plane backswing looks like, I've enlisted the help of PGA Tour player and former Ryder Cupper Jeff Overton, a student of mine since 2012. (Several of my Tour clients will help demonstrate my systems throughout this book.) Notice in the picture below how Overton's hands and clubhead stay very close to the circle from the start of his takeaway to the end of his backswing, and how he allows the clubface to rotate open to the point where the toe of the club is pointing toward the sky when he reaches the top. Combining an on-plane backswing with a neutral to open clubface is the key to being able to release the club correctly on the downswing (more on that in Fundamental No. 4). The net effect of this motion is greater versatility and better use of the bounce in tough lie conditions.

Jeff Overton's finesse backswing. Notice how both his hands and the clubhead travel on the shaft plane, and how his hips remain extremely stable. Check the logo on the side of his pants near his trail hip. It never moves.

Your Arm Swing Is Key

To nail the backswing and get both the handle and the head of the club moving up the plane simultaneously with the toe rotating open, you need to come to terms with two specific arm movements. The first is to maintain the cup that you establish in your lead wrist at address all the way to the top. If it disappears, you'll likely be "under" plane and in danger of poor contact. The second is to allow your trail arm to fold at the elbow as it externally rotates, which is clockwise if you play right-handed. Everything is essentially moving on the circle: the clubhead, your hands, and your trail elbow. These moves may sound complicated, but that's only because you're unfamiliar with the terminology. The following drill will make it seem like second nature.

Single-Arm Swing Drill

STEP 1: Get into your finesse address position (you can perform this drill without a ball). Take your trail hand off the grip and put it on your trail hip. Check that your lead wrist is still cupped. Swing the club straight back and up with your lead arm. As you do, keep an eye on your lead wrist and maintain its cup the whole way. This is what correct lead-arm movement feels like in a finesse swing.

STEP 2: Go back to your setup. Reverse the drill by placing your lead hand on your lead thigh while gripping the club with your trail hand only. Swing your trail hand back up the plane circle without allowing your elbow to separate from your side. You'll sense that your elbow must fold and your arm must rotate (clockwise) to keep the clubhead on the circle with the toe pointing skyward. Congratulations! You just experienced external rotation and the perfect trail-arm movement for a finesse backswing.

Of course, you need both arms to work correctly and in unison when you swing. An effective way to blend their respective actions is to practice in front of a full-length mirror. Set up to an imaginary ball with any of your wedges and the mirror positioned to your right (or your left if you're a left-handed golfer), giving you a down-the-line view of your finesse setup and swing. Then, turn your head toward the mirror. Note the shaft's position in the reflection and then slowly swing back. If your arm movements are correct, the club will crawl up the shaft line and the toe of the club will rotate toward the sky. If either the handle or the clubhead deviate from the shaft line, start over. Keep at it—this is invaluable feedback. A great checkpoint occurs when the shaft is parallel to the ground. Here, it should look like the shaft is pointing parallel to the target line, with the toe up and the clubhead hiding your hands.

Champions Tour player Tom Pernice Jr. nailing an important checkpoint in the finesse wedge swing. When the shaft is horizontal in the backswing, it points parallel to the target line, with the toe pointing up and the clubhead "hiding" his hands.

Matters of Style

I've coached PGA Tour Players Tom Pernice Jr. and Charlie Wi since 1996. I've armed them with the same information, same practice drills, and same fundamentals, but their finesse wedge swings don't look all that similar (at least to the untrained eye). That's because they've applied their own style to their finesse swing, which is certainly acceptable as long as you don't deviate from the five fundamentals. You can turn your upper body very little in the backswing and therefore have a narrower arc and more wrist hinge (like Pernice, and Seve back in the day), or you could favor more upper-body rotation so that your arms stay in front of you (like Wi). The first style looks a little free and wristy, while the second looks more dead-handed, but it's possible to trace the ideal plane and deliver the club correctly with either. It's simply a matter of what makes you feel most comfortable and in control.

FINESSE WEDGE FUNDAMENTAL NO. 3: USE A FINESSE SEQUENCE

Great setups and backswings fuel the *potential* for success, but there's still the matter of your downswing, and without the right information, it's easy to fall off track. I'll start your downswing lesson by quoting a paragraph from my *Short Game Notebook*:

"The downswing necessitates nothing more than letting the club fall back to the ground in a circle as if pulled by gravity, and letting your chest rotate to support the motion of the swing. There's a natural weight shift, or energy flow, toward the target as the lower body remains level and relatively quiet until the club passes it, allowing the clubhead to release under its own momentum."

Sounds pretty tame, doesn't it? That's because it is! It's finesse—the smooth-flowing sequence of downswing events that makes great wedge players great and the rest just mediocre. It's what I saw in the video from the Players Championship and what I've preached every day since. Having a feel for the right sequence of movement in order to get the club and ball to do what you want them to do is critical to being great around the greens.

As mentioned in Chapter 1, the Titleist Performance Institute has used computer-mapping technology to measure what, when, and how fast everything moves in relation to everything else during the swing. Science has quantified exactly what the best players in the world do to both generate power and great ball flight, not to mention produce those magical shots around the green. Swing sequence is critical because it affects the speed of your swing, the location of the bottom of your arc, and the effective loft and bounce of your club. Even though different sequences do exist in the short game, the ones recognized as the best of the best (i.e., Luke Donald, Tom Pernice Jr., Padraig Harrington, Corey Pavin, and Steve Stricker) all have the exact same 3-D kinematic sequence pattern. You can't argue it—it's fact.

In an efficient power swing (see photo below), the hips reach maximum speed first and then decelerate to pass their energy to the torso. Then the torso decelerates, passing energy to the arms, which decelerate to ultimately pass energy to the hands and the clubhead. This kinematic sequence is undisputed in golf teaching and research. In contrast, a finesse downswing begins with a slight casting motion in which the club moves earlier and faster than the arms, and then the torso and arms immediately outpace the hips. This is the opposite of what you do in your full swing.

Power sequence.

Notice in the finesse sequence how I initiate my downward movement by moving the club first, before my body. Think of it as a gentle casting motion or, to quote my *Notebook*, "letting gravity be your friend." You can see how my hips don't really turn until after the club gets back in front of my body.

Finesse sequence.

In a finesse swing the feeling you're after is that your arms are soft and re-laxed as they smoothly swing the clubhead past your lower body while your chest catches their momentum and rotates toward the target at the same pace.

The role of your lower body changes completely for a short shot. It's no longer a power generator, but a provider of stability and balance. If you hit your driver this way, the ball would go nowhere. A finesse sequence is inefficient for creating speed, but optimal for controlling it. Essentially, great wedge players are weak on purpose.

The lesson: reverse your swing sequence for better contact and touch around the greens and save your power sequence for the tee box.

The Lexicon of Wedge Play

Thanks to outfits such as Titleist Performance Institute, science has proven that power and club performance are largely determined by how you sequence your downswing. Therefore, I think we can do the golf world a favor and ditch the archaic terms "chipping" and "pitching." To me, these words entice players to use different arm swings to control distance and trajectory—there's only one correct arm swing movement. Plus, they say nothing about sequence. My suggestion is to replace chipping with "finesse wedge" and pitching with "distance wedge." You're either going to be in a finesse mode or a power mode, depending on the speed requirement of the shot and what you want the ball to do. By using these terms you'll automatically prioritize the correct movement. Everybody's ability to generate speed is different, but let's use 30 yards to the green as a rough cutoff point; anything inside 30 yards is a finesse wedge and anything 30 yards or longer is a distance wedge or mini-power swing.

FINESSE WEDGE FUNDAMENTAL NO. 4: LET THE CLUBHEAD RELEASE

Most players know that bounce is a design feature intended to prevent the clubhead from digging into the turf, but they aren't really sure how to make it work for them. That's because they incorrectly believe that they're supposed to keep their hands ahead of the clubhead throughout the downswing. Unfortunately, this unnatural move ruins the way the club interacts with the turf, causing it to dig and creating a domino effect of other technical problems. I'm amazed at the widespread use of this technique, and the alarming number of teachers who preach it.

On more than one occasion, Titleist master wedge designer Bob Vokey has told me, "Bounce is your friend." The only way to unlock its benefits is to let the clubhead pass your hands through impact so that more of the sole comes in contact with the turf.

Now, before you start flipping the club like you're cooking flapjacks on a Saturday morning, understand that letting the clubhead release is more the result of gravity than effort. The correct mindset and motion to effectively use the bounce is as follows:

1. Remain tension-free in your setup and throughout your swing. Let the club feel "heavy" in your hands.
2. As you transition from backswing to downswing, do it slowly and let gravity and the weight of the club conspire to drop the clubhead down the shaft plane.
3. Through impact, swing the clubhead naturally and past your hands into a great finish position.

To see what the proper release and finish position look like, check the sequence of PGA Tour player and student James Driscoll below. Notice in frame 1 how the shaft points at the middle of a triangle formed by his shoulders and arms just past impact. Here, the clubhead is even with his hands, but in the next frame it's way ahead—*gasp!* Also, notice that the clubface is open or pointed skyward in the finish (frame 3). This is evidence that the trail arm has rotated clockwise through impact, which is the dead opposite of what happens in the power swing. This "open-to-open" release of the clubhead allows Driscoll to simply brush the grass under the ball because the *sole* contacts the turf, not the leading edge. If you can do this, you can say good-bye to the debilitating chili-dip for good.

Using the bounce of the club produces minimal ground interference (no divot necessary in a finesse swing), which allows you to swing down into the turf without concern. Even if you accidently hit a little behind the ball, it will still go up in the air and end up next to the hole, increasing your margin of error and decreasing your stress level.

Like all great wedge players, PGA Tour player James Driscoll allows the clubhead to pass his hands through impact. Along with an on-plane delivery, this so-called "mistake" is one of the secrets to producing crisp, dig-free contact.

Good wedge players never look unnatural or "flippy" because they turn their chest to support the release of the club. As they move into the finish, they remain tension-free, allowing their lead elbow to fold and rotate around their side, and their lead wrist to extend or cup. Remember those wrinkles.

Tom Pernice Jr. demonstrating a picture-perfect finesse wedge finish. The clubhead has passed his hands, his lead elbow has folded and moved around his side, and his lead wrist has increased its cup.

The Best Drill I Know

Looking at pictures of the correct release is one thing, but you have to get a feel for it in order to reap its benefits. One of my favorite exercises—for this fundamental and for finesse wedge play in general—is to hit short shots using only your trail arm. I call it the Trail-Arm-Only Drill. I know it sounds simplistic, but it's a powerful drill. Hitting solid shots this way automatically creates the correct sequence and release in your swing, without any thinking on your part. Follow these steps:

1. Get into your finesse setup.

2. Take your lead hand off the grip and rest it on your front thigh.

3. Swing your trail arm back, keeping the club and handle on the shaft plane. Remember to rotate your arm clockwise and fold your elbow!

4. From the top, get the clubhead moving earlier and faster than your arms. Support this movement with chest rotation and ultimately by allowing your hips to turn.

5. Continue to swing your right arm past your lower body and smoothly accelerate the clubhead past your hands. It's critical that you turn your chest through impact to support the arm swing and allow the club to stay in front of you. Freeze your finish position. You know you did it correctly if the grip points at your belly and the face is slightly open.

6. Lastly, regrip the club with your lead hand and take note of how this requires you to both fold your lead elbow and move it around the side of your torso. When you're done, you'll notice that your lead wrist is cupped, just like it should be.

FINESSE WEDGE FUNDAMENTAL NO. 5:
LET YOUR ENERGY FLOW TOWARD THE TARGET

One of the things I remember most about practicing wedge shots as a struggling mini-tour player was trying to keep my head still. I had been told this was important and it kind of made sense, but the video from the Players Championship showed the opposite. Good wedge players don't keep their head steady at all. They move it toward the target a few inches during the backswing in what's essentially a reverse weight shift; then they either keep their head still from that point on or move it even farther forward in the downswing. Obviously, if their head is moving that way, their weight is also shifting in the same direction.

Why would they do this? I didn't have an answer immediately, but after years of teaching and accumulating video of all types of players, a pattern became evident. Players who suffer poor contact often move their head away from the target when they swing, moving the low point of their swing arc along with it, an error that leads to fat and thin mis-hits. Conversely, players who strike the ball properly reverse-shift in the backswing, which steepens the delivery and gets their weight flowing toward the pin. This moves the swing's low point forward, producing ball-first contact.

The head movement and forward energy flow of Jeff Overton is typical of elite wedge players. You can see how much his head moves forward between address and the top of his backswing, and how it basically stays in place (yet remains forward) all the way into his release.

Expert at Work!

Watch how PGA Tour Player Jeff Overton finesses the ball close to the pin in a special video. Visit jsegolfacademy.com/index.php/jeff-overton.

I've never heard another coach teach this, but the video evidence is indisputable: Energy flowing to the pin during a finesse swing is a fundamental key for creating a crisp, controlled strike. For decades or longer, those with great touch around the green have developed this athletic move innately. A good way to get a feel for this forward energy flow is to toss a ball underhanded. Follow these steps.

DRILL: Energy Toss
Start in your finesse setup while holding a ball in your trail hand next to the grip. Let the club fall to the ground and place your lead arm behind your back. While keeping your lower body stable, swing your trail arm back. Use your athleticism to toss the ball underhanded toward the target—just a few yards will do. My guess is that you won't lean back and simply flip your wrist, but rather use your body to create momentum in the direction of your arm swing. Check where your weight is as you complete the motion. This is what it feels like to have your energy flowing toward the pin.

Moving energy toward the target by allowing your head to drift forward during your swing is an essential motor program on finesse shots. Always check that the majority of your weight is over your front foot when you complete your swing. If it isn't, your energy error will severely limit the quality of your contact.

FINESSE WEDGE JOURNAL ENTRY

In the finesse wedge section of your journal, title a page "Technical Commitments" and write down the five fundamentals of finesse wedge play presented in this chapter. Under each fundamental, make a few notes describing the moves and feels that make that fundamental easy to execute. Use words and phrases that make sense to you (see example below). These notes are critical for accelerating your improvement and commitment, and are a great resource if your finesse swing ever falters.

FINESSE WEDGES

TECHNICAL COMMITMENTS:

1. Set up for finesse
   Stack my body and point the flashlight on the ground in front of the ball.

2. Swing up the plane with an open face
   Maintain the cup in my lead wrist.

3. Use the finesse sequence
   Feel like the club moves first—keep the hips still!

4. Let the club release
   Feel like I'm doing the Trail-Arm-Only drill.

5. Energy flows to the pin
   Swing like you're tossing a ball.

CHAPTER 5

FINESSE WEDGE FLAWS AND FIXES

In a finesse swing, balancing the elements that affect the angle of attack is the key to consistent contact and a reliable short game.

The five fundamentals I laid out in the previous chapter offer a critical balance: There are two elements that steepen the angle of attack, two elements that shallow it, and a neutral element.

FUNDAMENTAL BALANCE OF MY FINESSE WEDGE SYSTEM

STEEPENS ANGLE OF ATTACK	NEUTRAL	SHALLOWS ANGLE OF ATTACK
Finesse setup Energy to the pin	On-plane swing	Finesse sequence Releasing the club

Consistent contact is nothing more than piecing together your setup and swing variables so that they blend together in a workable, repeatable method. There may be more than one way to do it, but it has to function. Like a small jigsaw puzzle, not every piece has to be the perfect shape, as long as it fits nicely with another piece of the puzzle. Getting the pieces to fit is essentially the art of teaching, and I coach everyone based on that principle. It is perfectly normal for a good player to have a small imperfection in their technique that shallows their swing, and then to develop (subconsciously or otherwise) a competing technical error that steepens it to create functionality—a makeup move, so to speak.

For some of my students, mastering the finesse wedge swing comes naturally. Others have to fight their way from the very start, and the majority fall somewhere in between. If you're a player who's suffering from poor contact, you have an imbalance of elements. For example, if you have an error where you set up with your head behind the ball (shallow), and then take the club inside the plane (shallow), your swing is going to be too shallow to produce good contact. In the same vein, if you take the clubhead outside-in the backswing (steep) then start your downswing with a power sequence (steep), you'll be too steep to perform well with any consistency.

You can't move forward into the finer areas of my Finesse Wedge System until you can execute the basic fundamentals. It's not always easy. At least one (and maybe more) may be counter to your current motor habits. Over the years, I've noticed that the same errors tend to crop up from student to student. Let's call them the common "fatal flaws" to finesse wedge play. Since I can't see if any of them exist in your swing, it's up to you to self-diagnose and correct them. Study the fourteen errors listed in this chapter one by one and think critically to see if they pertain to your motion. If they do, apply the appropriate fix (also listed). Note each error and fix in your journal. This will elevate the awareness of your swing and guide your practice so that you can manage your tendencies and rapidly improve.

The Fatal Flaws

FLAW NO. 1: Setting up for power, not finesse.
How you know you have it: Your upper body tilts away from the target.
Effect on angle of attack: Shallows it.
Effect on contact: Fat and thin shots.

NO!
Trail shoulder noticeably lower than lead shoulder.
Spine tilted away from the target.
Feet wide.
Chest square.
Head behind the ball.
Hands rotated counterclockwise (from the camera's point of view) on the handle (Vs pointing to right shoulder).

YES!
Shoulders level.
Chest pointing in front of the ball.
Feet narrow.
Head positioned in the middle of your body.
Trail hand rotated clockwise (from the camera's point of view) on the handle (V pointing to chin).

How to fix it: Practice with a putter grip.

Create a training club by replacing the grip on an old sand wedge with a traditional putter grip (one with a flat front). Review the finesse wedge setup guidelines and place your feet in a finesse stance. Set the thumb of your trail hand flat against the top of the grip so that it points straight down the handle. Getting your trail hand "on top" like this encourages you to "stack" your body over the ball at address with your chest open to the target so that your low point moves in front of the ball. (The putter grip is also a great way to feel how the toe of the club rotates open in the backswing. Simply make sure that the flat part of the putter grip is pointing skyward at the top, and the toe will do likewise.) Set up for finesse ten separate times as part of each practice session. Keep this club handy so you can work on your finesse setup as needed. Also see Fix No. 3: Stack Drill.

FLAW NO. 2: Setting your hands too far ahead of the clubhead at address.
How you know you have it: Your lead arm feels rigid and straight.
Effect on angle of attack: Steepens it.
Effect on contact: "Diggy" fat shots, low ball flight, little backspin.

NO!
Lead arm extended and tense.
Hands in front of lead thigh.
Shaft leaning dramatically toward the
    target.

YES!
Lead arm relaxed and slightly bent.
Hands in front of zipper.
Shaft leaning softly toward the target.

How to fix it: Use your reflection.

It should take you about two minutes to fix this common error. Set up in front of a full-length mirror and check that the ball is positioned just inside your trail foot. Keep your lead arm soft, and grip the club with your hands in front of your zipper. Do it right and the shaft will lean about 3 to 7 degrees toward the target. Make ten finesse wedge swings, checking your setup each time. At the beginning, address the ball while looking in the mirror to make sure you're setting up correctly. Near the end, check the mirror *after* you've addressed the ball. Ingrain the feeling; you won't have this luxury on the course.

FLAW NO. 3: Setting up with a closed chest or stance.

How you know you have it: The target feels like it's over your lead shoulder.

Effect on angle of attack: Shallows it.

Effect on contact: An ugly combination of fat and thin shots.

NO!
Both feet square to the target line.
Chest pointing at the ball.
Trail forearm "under" lead forearm.

YES!
Front foot pulled back slightly and
 flared toward the target.
Chest pointing in front of the ball.
Trail forearm even with lead forearm
 and pointing along your foot line.

How to fix it: Try my Stack Drill.

STEP 1: Set your feet in a finesse wedge position as you normally would, but instead of soling your wedge on the ground, hinge it up in front of you as though it's a fishing pole. Check that your trail-hand grip is on top and that your head is aligned with (or "stacked" over) the center of your sternum, belt buckle, and the middle of the space between your ankles.

STEP 2: Without losing your "stack," rotate your upper body slightly toward the target, as shown.

STEP 3: Maintain your body positioning and sole the club on the ground by bending forward from your hip joints. Voilà!—the perfect finesse wedge address position. Repeat ten times to ingrain the right feel.

FLAW NO. 4: Swinging back below the shaft plane with a closed face (*THE* fatal flaw).

How you know you have it: You hinge or increase the angle in the back of your trail wrist as you take the club away.

Effect on angle of attack: Shallows it.

Effect on contact: This is a huge error—expect the gamut of poor shots: fat and thin, double-hits, and in some cases, shanks.

NO!
Clubhead inside target line and closed.
Shaft below the plane it rested on at address.
Cup in lead wrist removed.

YES!
Clubhead directly over target line and slightly open.
Shaft on the same plane it rested on at address.
Cup in lead wrist maintained.

How to fix it: Try my Headcover Drill.

STEP 1: Set an alignment stick on the ground about two inches inside the ball (toward you). Make sure the stick point is parallel to the target line. Place one of your headcovers (or a rolled-up towel) on the stick and opposite your trail foot. Rehearse your backswing five times using the stick on the ground to guide the clubhead up the proper plane. As you complete the backswing, check to make sure you've maintained the cup in your lead wrist.

STEP 2: With that ingrained feeling, hit ten solid finesse wedge shots. A club that is taken up and then delivered on plane will easily miss the headcover. Also, see flaw No. 5: Follow your reflection.

FLAW NO. 5: Swinging back above the shaft plane.
How you know you have it: Your arms feel like they "separate" from your body during your backswing.
Effect on angle of attack: Steepens it.
Effect on contact: Creates fat shots, deep divots, and, in some cases, shanks.

NO!
Clubhead outside target line and closed.
Shaft above the plane it rested on at address.
Cup in lead wrist removed.

YES!
Clubhead on the target line and slightly open.
Shaft on the same plane it rested on at address.
Cup in lead wrist maintained.

How to fix it: Follow your reflection.

Position a mirror to your right (left for a left-handed player) and on an extension of your target line. Execute ten backswings in a row using only your lead arm. Track the movement of the club in your reflection, making sure it travels up the plane established by the shaft at address. It should be easy—the club is way too heavy to take back shut (closed) and outside using only your lead arm. Pause at the end of each backswing and add your trail hand to the grip. You may be surprised at how much your trail arm has to rotate clockwise for your trail hand to fit back on the handle, but this is the feel of the correct position. Practicing finesse shots outdoors using only your lead arm is a great way to train your finesse swing. It's Tom Pernice's go-to drill to create the feeling of the proper arm swing.

FLAW NO. 6: Turning your hips early in your backswing.

How you know you have it: You feel the club whip to the inside on your takeaway.

Effect on angle of attack: Shallows it.

Effect on contact: Creates thin shots and ground-first contact.

NO!
Hips turning away from the target.
Arms swinging inside the target line.
Clubhead pulled inside the shaft plane.

YES!
Hips still—no turn whatsoever.
Arms swinging straight back.
Club swinging up the shaft plane.

How to fix it: Try my Reverse Stork Drill.

Get into your finesse wedge setup, and then pull your lead foot back a foot or so and rest it on its toe. Swing back and keep your lower body quiet. Because you're balancing on one leg with your hips open, you'll lose your balance if you rotate your lower body. On your downswing, maintain lower-body stability and get the clubhead moving first. In the finish, turn your chest to support the arm swing and release the face open. Repeat ten times.

FLAW NO. 7: Closing the clubface during the backswing.

How you know you have it: Your trail arm is straight in the backswing.

Effect on angle of attack: Steepens it.

Effect on contact: "Diggy" low shots that don't spin very much.

NO!
Trail arm rotating counterclockwise.
Trail arm straight.
Clubface pointing at the ball.

YES!
Trail arm rotating clockwise.
Trail arm bending at the elbow.
Elbow moving on a slight arc up and
    around your side.
Toe of the club pointing toward the sky.

How to fix it: Try my Glove Drill.

STEP 1: Tuck your glove between your trail elbow and your rib cage, just above the elbow. Press your elbow tight enough against your rib cage to keep the glove in place. Your goal? Make a finesse wedge backswing without letting the glove fall to the ground. As you take the club back, keep your elbow in close while rotating your trail arm. If you rotate your trail arm the wrong direction (counterclockwise) or don't allow your trail elbow to fold, the glove will drop. Your swing should feel "narrow," with the clubhead rotating open and traveling up the shaft plane.

STEP 2: Let the club drop down the plane line and support its release with upper-body rotation. Don't worry if the glove falls near your finish. Repeat ten times.

FLAW NO. 8: Moving energy away from the target in the backswing.
How you know you have it: You feel your weight shifting slightly to your back foot.
Effect on angle of attack: Shallows it.
Effect on contact: Thin shots and hitting the ground behind the ball.

NO!
Upper body and head moving away
   from the target.
Weight on back foot.

YES!
Upper body and head moving toward
   the pin.
Weight on front foot.

How to fix it: Try my Shadow Drill.

STEP 1: Push an alignment stick in the ground so that it's straight up and down. With the sun at your back, get into your finesse wedge stance and shuffle your feet until the shadow cast by your head falls over the stick.

STEP 2: Using the stick as a reference, take the club back while looking at your shadow. If it moves behind the stick, you've allowed your energy to move away from the target. Not good. Repeat until your head's shadow moves slightly in front of the shaft during your backswing.

STEP 3: On your downswing, keep your shadow in the same place or move it even closer to the target. If you have difficulty performing this drill, check that your front foot is flared toward the target at address. This open-foot position allows your chest to remain relatively level as it rotates and supports the release of the club, keeping your head from falling back. Execute ten successful shadow swings.

FLAW NO. 9: Standing up through impact.

How you know you have it: Your weight moves from your heels in your setup to the balls of your feet as you near impact.

Effect on angle of attack: Shallows it.

Effect on contact: Creates off-center contact as well as dropkicks. It also makes it difficult to control distance.

NO!
Upper body rising up.
Hips thrusting inward toward the ball.
Weight moving toward the toes.
High hands at impact.

YES!
Impact posture the same as at address.
Hips back.
Weight moving toward the heels.
Hands returning to the same height as
setup position.

How to fix it: Try my Wall Balance Drill.

Losing your posture, or what instructors call "early extension," happens when you move your hips closer to the ball as the club nears impact. This raises the hands and drops the clubhead underneath them—a huge error. Your hips aren't the problem. It's your balance. If you set up with too much knee flex and your weight favoring your heels, your weight invariably will shift toward your toes as you swing into the ball, pulling your hips up and forward in the process. To fix this, set up with your back to a wall with straighter legs and a majority of your weight out toward the balls of your feet. Shuffle your stance until your rear end barely touches the wall behind you. Without a club, mimic a finesse wedge swing. Your goal is to keep your lead butt cheek in contact with the wall all the way to the finish. Repeat ten times to ingrain the feeling of the balance necessary to maintain posture.

FLAW NO. 10: Turning your hips too early as you start your downswing.

How you know you have it: It doesn't feel like you can square the face.

Effect on angle of attack: Shallows it.

Effect on contact: You'll hit weak undercut pushes out to the right, or drop-kicks.

NO!
Hips rotate before the club and arms start down.
Club "stuck" behind body.

YES!
Hips quiet at the start of the downswing.
Hands and club moving earlier and fastest.
Club on plane.

How to fix it: Try my Stork Drill.

Get into your finesse wedge setup, then pull your trail foot back a few inches and rest it on its toe. Swing back to the top of your backswing. Because you're balancing on your lead leg it will be difficult to rotate your hips as you start your downswing. If you do, you'll lose your balance. At the start of your downswing, focus on getting the clubhead moving first and on the feel of lower-body stability. Pose your finish and check that your chest has rotated more than your hips. This disassociation is a key look for those who've used the finesse sequence correctly. Repeat ten times.

FLAW NO. 11: "Down-cocking" your wrists at the start of the downswing.
How you know you have it: It feels like the clubhead is lagging behind your hands.
Effect on angle of attack: Steepens it.
Effect on contact: Produces fat and low shots that rob you of short-game touch.

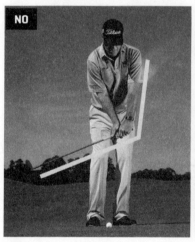
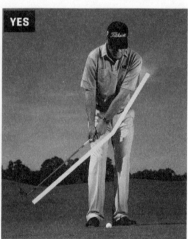

NO!
Power sequence causing wrist
  angles to increase.
Arms moving faster than the
  clubhead, creating extra
  downswing wrist hinge, the
  severity of which makes
  consistent contact impossible.

YES!
Wrists unhinging perfectly.
Clubhead moving earlier and
  faster than the arms,
  "letting out" wrist and arm
  angles at the start of your
  downswing.

How to fix it: Try my Trail-Arm-Only Drill.

Very few mistakes are more destructive than transitioning from backswing to downswing with poor sequencing, particularly when you move your lead arm faster than the club. This produces "down-cock," or an increase in wrist hinge at the start of the downswing, which is good for power but destructive for finesse. Repeat the Trail-Arm-Only Drill from page 39. Hit ten shots, focusing on your tempo during the transition segment of your swing. If you sequence for finesse, the club will move earlier and fall faster than the lead arm. If it feels like you're gently "casting" the club, you're doing it correctly.

FLAW NO. 12: Moving energy away from the target during the downswing.
How you know you have it: You finish your swing in a "fall-back" motion.
Effect on angle of attack: Shallows it.
Effect on contact: Creates ground contact behind the ball, fat and thin shots, and dropkicks.

NO!
Upper body and head moving away
  from the target.
Weight on back foot.

YES!
Upper body and head moving toward
  the target.
Weight on front foot.

How to fix it: Try my Squash Drill.

Place something soft, such as an energy bar, under the heel of your trail foot at address, making sure to just barely rest your foot on top of it. Your goal is to make your finesse wedge swing without crushing the bar. This drill creates awareness regarding balance and will force you to make an athletic movement in which energy flows toward the target in your downswing. Note: Many people who move their head or upper body away from the target in the downswing are compensating for a closed clubface in the backswing, so double-check the face angle at the top of your backswing and correct it if necessary. Also perform the Shadow Drill from pages 56 and 57.

FLAW NO. 13: "Flipping" the clubhead through impact.
How you know you have it: You rarely produce that audible *thump* sound of crisp contact.
Effect on angle of attack: Shallows it.
Effect on contact: Thin shots, and high-trajectory shots that come up short.

NO!
Arms and chest decelerating before impact.
Clubhead "flipping" past the hands.

YES!
Arms and chest accelerating past impact.
Chest pointing at the target in the finish.
Butt end of club pointing to the belly button.

How to fix it: Try my Coin Drill.

From a tight fairway lie, place a dime on the ground about three inches in front of the ball, on your target line. At address, visualize hitting both the ball and the coin onto the green, then see if you can do it. Using external cues like hitting the dime are often the easiest way to quickly implement changes. If you allow your lead arm to decelerate prior to impact and flip the clubhead at the ball, you'll miss the coin every time. It's important to know that the "flip" is not the problem, but the effect of the problem. The real issue is the premature deceleration of your arms and chest. Support the release by accelerating them past impact. This will keep the energy moving toward the target and stop you from flipping.

FLAW NO. 14: "Blocking" the release of the clubhead.

How you know you have it: Your lead arm stays straight and is filled with tension.

Effect on angle of attack: Steepens it.

Effect on contact: Fat shots, deep divots, low ball flight, and poor touch.

NO!

Lead arm tense, locked straight, and off the body.

Hands leading the clubhead.

Butt end of the club pointing up to the sky.

YES!

Lead arm soft and close to torso.

Clubhead releasing naturally past the hands.

Butt end of the club pointing at the belly button.

How to fix it: Pose for the camera.

This one's easy—relax your hands and arms throughout your finesse wedge swing and hold your finish position. Your finish holds hidden clues about the overall quality of your swing, especially in the way you allow the club to release through impact. If you're not hitting the positions shown in the photo on the next page, then you're fighting nature and not allowing the club to release correctly.

A. Chest facing the target.

B. Clubface open and butt of the club pointing at your belly button.

C. Arms tension-free, with the elbows in close to the torso.

D. Weight has flowed into the lead foot.

E. Lower body providing stability and aiding in balance.

THE "SIXTH" FUNDAMENTAL

The drills listed in this chapter will prove instrumental in your development of a finesse wedge swing that consistently produces solid contact. But there's still the matter of tempo, or the rhythm of your swing. All great wedge players have a flowing rhythm to their motion. Without this flow you'll have difficulty controlling shot distance, even with solid contact. If your swing feels more jerky than smooth, the following three drills will show you how to swing with better rhythm.

One-And-Two Drill: Set up for a practice swing next to your ball. While looking at your landing spot, swing to the beat of the following count: Say "One" as you make the backswing, "And" at the top of your backswing (which will give you a slight pause), and "Two" as you swing through the ball. Now look at your ball, visualize the landing spot and swing to the count again. As you finish the second practice swing, imagine the ball flying perfectly to the pin. Immediately address the ball, give your target one last look and then swing with the same "One-And-Two" cadence. PGA Tour player Charlie Wi does this on every finesse swing. (See if you can spot him doing it the next time you see him on TV.) This technique not only perfects your rhythm, it also helps you mentally engage with the target.

Finger-Off Drill: Take your normal finesse grip, but then move your hands up the handle until the pinkie finger of your lead hand is completely off the grip. Lift the club slowly off the ground a quarter-inch at a time until it feels "heavy" in your hands. With this heavy feel fresh in your mind, make a finesse wedge swing, maintaining light grip pressure the whole way. Remember that there are no jerky moves in a great finesse swing, and that gravity is your friend. Repeat ten times.

Pause Drill: Set up for a shot and make your normal finesse wedge backswing. Pause at the top for two seconds. Start your downswing while focusing on moving the club first and accelerating in a smooth, unrushed manner. Execute ten successful shots. Most rhythm mistakes are caused from tension and a quick transition.

Perfecting Your Release

One key to having a rhythmic swing is allowing the club to release freely past your hands through the hitting area. I know you're trying, but how do you know you have it exactly right and aren't either flipping the club or blocking it? You can check the quality of your release by studying the way the club makes contact with the ground. If you hear a solid *thump* at impact (the sound of the sole hitting the ground) and barely disturb the grass, you're releasing the club nicely. If you tend to dig the leading edge into the turf and extract sizable divots, you're not. In this case, perform the Glove Drill (page 55) and work on letting the clubface rotate open in your backswing. Perform the Trail-Arm-Only Drill (page 39) to work on smoothing out your transition and getting the clubhead moving earlier and faster than your arm on your downswing. It's nearly impossible to hang onto your release swinging with only your trail arm. If you're a digger, it will give you the feeling you need for a natural, fundamentally solid release.

For those of you who would like to be more specific and measure your release, you'll need the help of a video camera. Film yourself from a face-on perspective. Draw a line over the shaft at your address position. Draw a second, parallel line just in front of the first (see photo below). Step the video forward through impact. If you release the club like a pro, the shaft will cover or match the second line just after impact. If the club is leaning away from the target at this point, you've "flipped" the clubhead. If the handle is leading the clubhead at this point, then you're "hanging on." Performing this exercise will prove that even though you're releasing the club and using the bounce, the clubhead still slightly *descends* into the ball.

PGA Tour player James Driscoll's shaft position at impact is slightly ahead of its position at address. Other than that, it's a perfect copy, which is evidence that the club is releasing perfectly and not being held off or flipped.

Dare I Mention the Yips?

If you think you have the chipping yips, relax—you likely don't have the real neurological condition known as *focal dystonia*. Rather, you likely suffer from performance anxiety caused by coupling dysfunctional technique with an emotional attachment to the outcome. In other words, you're experiencing horrible results and it bothers you. The good news is that your problem is solvable. Every player who has come to me in this condition over the last twenty years has been under the plane and shut in the backswing, complete with makeup moves like poor sequencing and a leg buckle to try to move the low point of their swing forward. A club that's delivered from the inside is too shallow to produce ball-first contact except on an upslope or when the ball is teed up in the rough; a closed clubface causes the club to dig into the turf. This we know: Digging the club into the turf behind the ball isn't good for your score or your psyche.

Performance anxiety creates real physiological problems, which often persist even after your technique improves. You'll need to do some mental training, but the first step to recovery is to get the club up and open in the backswing so that it can be delivered to the ball without manipulation. Start with the Head-cover (page 51), Glove (page 55), and Trail-Arm-Only (page 39) drills, and keep at them until you can execute all three competently in training. The combination of these drills will ensure that you're delivering the club on plane and not from under it with a closed face. They'll also ingrain the correct sequence for finesse and the proper release so you can use the bounce of the club. It's impossible to have the yips if you do these three things.

PGA Tour Confidential: Ben Crane

"I know that when I get off track, my technique is usually changing in response to setup errors. So the first thing I do is pull out my alignment stick and go through all my address-position checks. Once I know I'm set up correctly, I work on the feel of what it's like to swing back and deliver the club on plane. When I first started with James, I bowed my lead wrist during my backswing and swung the clubhead under the shaft plane. This forced me to drive my legs toward the target to move the low point of my swing forward so I didn't hit behind the ball. These errors made for inconsistent contact and touch. James got me making twenty swings in front of a mirror at least once a day on off weeks, watching and getting a feel for the club moving up the plane with a slight cup in my left wrist. When I'm at a Tour event, I'll repeat my setup checks and hit shots into an open space, constantly focusing on the cup in my lead wrist and my tempo in the transition of the swing. If the contact isn't there, I'll perform James's Coin Drill, which always gets me hitting crisp shots."

JOURNAL WORK

In the finesse wedge section of your journal, write down your flaw tendencies and the drills you can do—and the feels you can use—to fix them.

FINESSE WEDGES

MY FLAWS & MY FIXES:

1. "Down-cocking" and losing rhythm by starting down too quickly, which is why I occasionally chunk the turf and my good shots often go too far.

- *Relax my arms and feel a heavy club.*
- *Trail-Arm-Only Drill (page 39) to train the sequence.*
- *One-and-Two Drill (page 66) at least twice a week to get in a rhythm.*

2. I tend to set up too square with my chest and forearms, so I take the club a little inside instead of up the plane.

- *During the winter, check setup in basement mirror every week.*
- *During the season, point my "flashlight" in front of the ball. Make it part of my pre-shot routine when I address the ball.*

CHAPTER 6

FINESSE WEDGE SKILL DEVELOPMENT AND ADAPTATIONS

Being able to see a shot, judge your lie, and apply the appropriate adjustments so you can pull it off is truly the "art of golf."

S uccessfully applying the finesse wedge fundamentals presented thus far will certainly result in great contact, but there's a lot more to being great than that. What happens when you have an odd lie or need to change the trajectory? What happens when your solid shots roll too far past the pin? Beyond having great technique, great wedge players know how to select the appropriate shot, visualize landing spots, manipulate shot trajectory, as well as effectively judge and adapt to different lie conditions. These are *skills*—the talented application of knowledge and advanced moves that build on the five fundamentals and allow you to handle anything the course throws at you. Here are the keys to developing them and transforming your finesse wedge swing into a legitimate scoring weapon.

HOW TO CONTROL FINESSE WEDGE TRAJECTORY

Within the structure of my Finesse Wedge System are two effective ways to control trajectory or hit the "trajectory window" you visualize in your pre-shot routine. The first and most obvious one is to vary your club selection. All things being equal, less-lofted clubs (your 9-iron, for example) produce lower trajectories and less spin than higher-lofted clubs (i.e., your sand wedge). In addition, you can create different trajectories with the same club by making changes to your setup. By moving the ball back in your stance and keeping your hands hanging over your

Change trajectories by switching to a higher- or lower-lofted club, or vary the shaft lean and face angle of the clubhead at address. Whatever adaptions you choose, there's only one arm motion, and it always stays the same.

zipper, the shaft will lean more toward the target. This reduces loft, which lowers trajectory. The opposite happens when you move the ball up in your stance while keeping your hands hanging in the same place, the shaft will move vertically, creating more loft and a higher trajectory. (For even higher shots, you can rotate the clubface open as well.) This will give you a minimum of three trajectories with each club. The good news is that the fundamental rules of the finesse wedge swing you've already learned still apply. Regardless of the club you use or the trajectory you choose, you always set up for finesse, swing on plane with a finesse sequence, and release the club with your energy flowing toward the target.

Notice in the photos on the preceding page how shaft lean decreases and effective loft increases as I move the ball from off my back foot (frame 1, lower than normal shot) to up between my toes (frame 3, higher than normal shot). An important key is that the more forward you play the ball in your stance, the more you need to open your chest to the target at address so that your sternum is always pointing to a spot on the ground a few inches in front of the ball. This helps get the low point of your swing in front of the ball, even with a forward ball position.

For an extremely high shot (preceding page, bottom right image), create maximum loft by setting up as though you're hitting a bunker shot (this will be covered in Chapter 10). Stand farther away from the ball, widen your stance and lower your hands to almost knee height. As you drop your hands, allow the clubface to rotate open. Even though it's a completely different stance than what you've seen so far, it requires the same finesse wedge motion as the others (and perhaps a longer, faster arm swing).

Expert at Work!

Watch how PGA Tour Player Cameron Tringale varies finesse wedge trajectory in a special video. Visit jsegolfacademy.com/index.php/cameron-tringale.

HOW TO DEVELOP FINESSE WEDGE TOUCH AND DISTANCE CONTROL

In the short game, it's relatively easy to hit it straight (unlike the power game), so the most valuable skill is learning to control your distance. Distance control, or "touch," is a function of the effective loft of the club at impact, the impact conditions, and the player's ability to sense how much energy must be imparted to the ball to get it pin high. There's a certain level of judgment involved, but in techni-

SWING LENGTH VS. ENERGY
Alter swing length—not its rhythm—to vary shot distance: Make a longer swing for more energy on longer wedge shots and a shorter swing for less energy on shorter wedge shots. Always match the length of your backswing with the length of your throughswing.

cal terms you control energy with swing length and rhythm. When you swing in rhythm, your backswing and the downswing match on both sides of impact, you appear flowing and graceful (the finesse sequence will help), and it will take the same amount of time to complete your swing regardless of its length. As such, your short wedge swings—for shorter finesse wedge shots—will feel "slower" than your big wedge swings (i.e., the ones you use for longer finesse wedge shots).

Every golfer has his or her innate rhythm. What's good for me or for one of my Tour players may not be good for you. There isn't one "perfect" pace. Some players are naturally brisk; Tom Watson and Brandt Snedeker come to mind. Others, like Steve Stricker, are more languid. Your rhythm is your own, and it should never change. To find it, repeat the One-and-Two Drill from page 66, saying "one-and-two" in a rhythmic manner while you swing. Having great rhythm allows you to swing past the ball and not "hit" at it. It's the key to developing great touch.

Given the lie conditions, the effective loft of the club you've chosen, and your natural rhythm, there's only one swing length that'll impart the correct amount of energy to the ball to stop it pin high. To find it, get lost mentally in the shot as you set up. Look at the target while swinging rhythmically next to the ball, and establish a feel for the swing length that matches the energy your mind tells you is necessary for the shot at hand. Once you have it, step in and react to that picture.

HOW TO ASSESS LIES IN THE ROUGH

Even though every situation is different, there are essentially two types of lies in the rough: "clean" lies and "fluff" lies. As the descriptions indicate, a clean lie allows you to get the clubface on the back of the ball with no real grass interference—like a shot from the fairway. In this case, no adaptation is needed and you can play a normal shot.

Fluff lies are a different matter, and the trick is determining how much the grass behind the ball will influence the shot. USGA rules forbid you from testing the surface around your lie, so you can't press your club into the ground or push grass away from the ball. You can, however, set your club lightly behind the ball and "measure the fluff." This act will make it fairly easy to determine if you'll be able to get the clubface cleanly on the back of the ball and, if not, the amount of grass that will come between the clubface and the ball at impact. Judging how much influence the fluff will have on an ensuing shot is critical to performance. Use the following criteria:

1. *Check for Moisture*
   Seve Ballesteros taught my brother, Tom, to determine the moisture content of the grass around and underneath the ball. The wetter the grass, the

more energy it will take out of your swing, mandating a longer, faster motion. The dryer the grass, the less it will affect the energy.

2. *Check the Grain*

If the grain (the direction in which the grass is growing) is lying in your favor (toward the target), then the ball should fly out normally, as if from a clean lie. If the grain direction is coming toward you, it will exert a dramatic effect and require a longer swing and more energy. When I'm out coaching on Tour and locate a spot around the short-game practice area with this kind of into-the-grain fluffy lie, I'll bet the player $5 that they come up short. Ultimately, it's a good lesson for them, and it never hurts to have a little extra gas money on my end.

3. *Check the Density*

Density deals with both the thickness of the grass blades and how close they're growing together, which is species dependent. Thick grasses such as Kikuyu, fescue, Bermuda, and bent (which often seeps from the green and fairway into the rough) sap the most energy from your intended swing. Less dense grasses such as bluegrass and winter rye have less of an effect.

To extricate your ball from a clean lie in the rough, use your standard finesse wedge setup and swing. To hit it crisply from a fluff lie, you'll need to adjust your setup to create a steeper angle of attack and add energy.

Once you determine that you have a fluff lie and consider the factors regarding the severity of its influence, you need to counteract it by steepening your angle of attack, which encourages the club to work up the plane more abruptly. How do you steepen the angle? Easy—create it with your address position by making the following adjustments: widen your stance, choke down on the club to the bottom of the grip, and lean a little extra weight into your lead thigh, which will allow your upper body and the handle of the club to slide toward the target. (The parameters for controlling trajectory remain the same.) Creating angle will make a huge difference in the quality of your contact, but you may also have to ramp up the energy depending on the severity of the lie by making a bigger swing. Remember, in the finesse game, you increase swing length, not rhythm, to add energy. Don't confuse "bigger swing" with "hit it harder."

HOW TO FINESSE FROM DEEP ROUGH

STEP 1: Choke down, widen out, and "lean" your weight into your lead thigh (all other finesse fundamentals apply).

STEP 2: These setup adjustments create a steeper, narrower backswing arc.

STEP 3: Maintain the pressure in your lead leg as you deliver the club with a steeper angle of attack. This will minimize grass interference and produce crisp ball/club contact.

HOW TO ADJUST FOR SLOPES

Creating angle at address isn't the only way to alter your angle of attack. You can also do it by changing your swing plane, an asset that comes in handy when you're faced with the challenge of hitting finesse wedges off upslopes and downslopes and with the ball either above or below your feet. Delivering the club from inside the target line shallows your angle of attack, while swinging outside-in (more "across the ball") steepens it. Depending on the slope on which the ball is resting, adjusting the plane one way or the other will make a big difference in the quality of your contact.

1. Downslopes

The perfect clubhead angle of attack into the ball is 6 degrees for a standard lie. If your ball is resting on a downslope with, say, a 4-degree grade, you'll need 10 degrees of attack angle to hit the shot crisply (4 degrees for the grade plus the standard 6-degree attack). If you fail to make any adjustments to your setup or swing in this situation, you'll come in too shallow, either striking the ground behind the ball or skulling the shot across the green. How do you add 4 degrees of attack angle to maintain the effective angle of 6? You create it at address by widening your stance, choking down to the bottom of the grip, and leaning down the hill as shown in the photos on the next page. In addition, shift your plane a little more out-to-in. On downslopes, think "fade" not "draw."

HOW TO FINESSE FROM A DOWNSLOPE:

STEP 1: Widen your stance, lean into your lead leg, and choke down on the handle.

STEP 2: Let the club work up more abruptly in your backswing. A swing that's too shallow will lead to dumpy little chunks or skulled shots across the green.

STEP 3: Shift your swing plane a tad out-to-in by thinking "fade."

STEP 4: Maintain pressure into your lead thigh the whole way.

2. *Upslopes*

Uphill lies naturally increase your effective angle of attack, so if you have a fluff lie you don't have to do anything more than add energy to your swing to hit a successful shot. On a clean lie, however, you need to execute with a bit of a "draw" mentality. I call this my "Raymond Floyd Shot," because it mimics his distinct setup and swing. Open your stance more than normal at address and make a backswing that feels a little inside, or "laid off." Even though this swing is inside-out relative to your body, it's still delivering the clubhead in line with the target, which will help the ball fly straight. The Raymond Floyd specialty shot also works well for a ball that happens to be teed up in the rough (sitting on top of the grass like a snow cone). In addition to swinging with a draw feel, select a less-lofted club. If executed properly, it'll feel like you're picking the ball off the grass.

HOW TO FINESSE FROM AN UPSLOPE (HIT THE "RAYMOND FLOYD"):

STEP 1: Open your stance more than normal.

STEP 2: Take the club back a little to the inside.

STEP 3: Think "draw" to create a shallower, inside-out swing that will allow you to maintain the ideal angle of attack and catch the ball solidly.

3. Sideslopes

You'll also get lies in which the ball is below or above your feet. Balls below your feet require a fade mentality in your setup and swing. Fades go short, so remember to add a little energy to your motion. In addition, widen your stance and get as close to the ball as possible. The shaft will sit a little more vertical than normal. That's OK—it'll stop the heel of the club from catching the turf first.

For a ball above your feet, face alignment is critical. When you sole on the ground with the scoring lines square to the target, the loft of the club actually closes the face, despite its appearance. The first adjustment is to "aim the face, not the lines on it" at the landing area. The face will appear to open and increase in loft as you do this, but the ball will fly toward the target. Remember to add energy to your swing and shallow your angle of attack by taking the club back a little to the inside.

Desired Angle of Attack on Common Short-Game Lies

		LIE CONDITION		
		Tight	Clean Rough	Fluff Rough
SLOPE	Level	Neutral	Neutral	Steep
	Down	Steep	Steep	Steepest
	Up	Shallow	Shallow	Neutral
	Ball Above Feet	Shallow	Shallow	Shallow
	Ball Below Feet	Steep	Steep	Steepest

HOW TO FINESSE YOUR WAY OUT OF TROUBLE

When it comes to hitting finesse wedges around the green, I want you to feel like you have a shot for every conceivable lie and situation, adopt an offensive mindset, and then try to hole *everything*. In addition to your stock finesse wedge swing and the adjustments needed to alter trajectory and produce great contact from poor lies, it's helpful to add two additional specialty shots to your arsenal.

1. The Putt-Chip

As the name suggests, this swing is dominated by your big muscles and features little hand and wrist action. As a result, it produces a very shallow angle of attack and minimal energy, limiting the putt-chip to situations that require short carries (less than 7 yards) and clean lies. It's ideal when the fairway is too sticky to putt through or when you're hitting from a lie that's muddy, sandy, or tight and into the grain.

MY FIVE FINESSE WEDGE SYSTEM FUNDAMENTALS:

1. Set up for finesse by establishing the low point of your swing arc in front of the ball.
2. Swing the club back up the plane with the toe rotated skyward.
3. Use the finesse sequence for soft touch and solid contact.
4. Let the club release so that you can use and benefit from the bounce on the club.
5. Allow energy to flow naturally toward the target.

TOM PERNICE JR. • FINESSE WEDGE SWING

Note how finesse-wedge master Tom Pernice Jr. sets up with his chest open and his lead foot flared out toward the pin. He cups his lead wrist during the backswing as much as anybody,

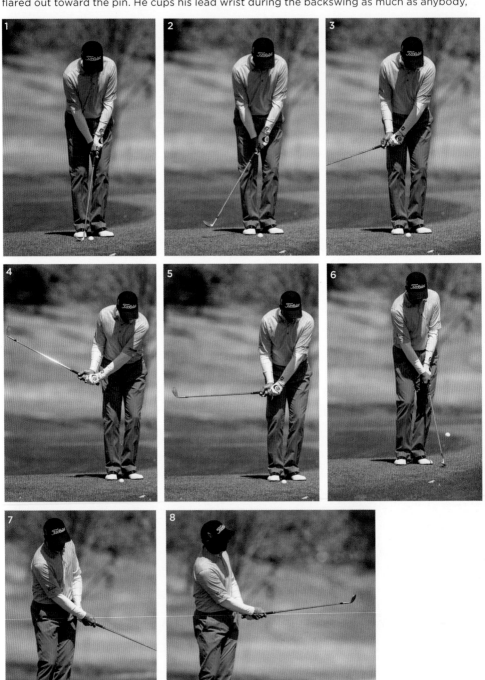

allowing him to release the clubhead with vigor at the bottom of his swing. Because of his impeccable rhythm and soft arms, he always looks graceful throughout his motion and into a balanced finish.

CHARLIE WI • GREENSIDE BUNKER SWING

Charlie Wi's bunker contact is always crisp and he has amazing control. I love his wide stance and the stability he creates by rotating both his feet outward in the setup. When he releases

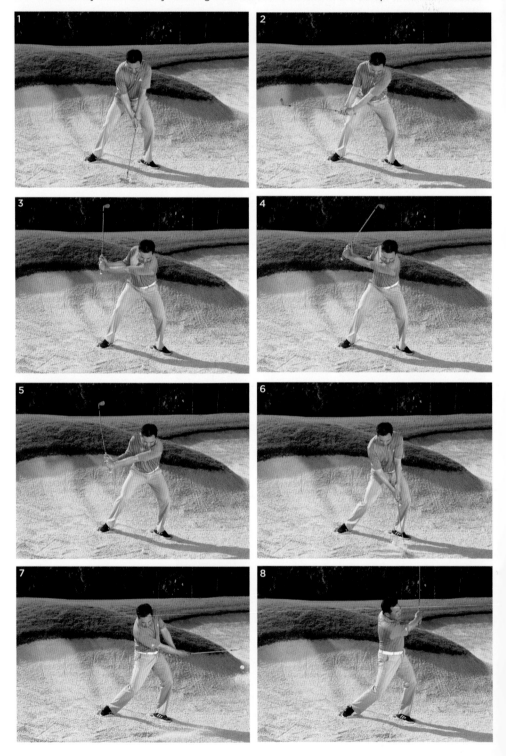

the clubhead past the ball, he adds flex and weight into his lead thigh and maintains the flex all the way into the finish. This is the telltale sign of a player who knows how to correctly thump the sand with speed.

BEN CRANE • DISTANCE WEDGE SWING

There's not a lot of wasted motion in Crane's distance wedge swing, which is why it's so efficient and why he's able to produce any yardage, any time. Notice how his head and center of balance stay in place as he hits his nine o'clock benchmark in the backswing. Perfect. He

delivers the club on an ideal path and uses his body to "cover" the ball for pure contact. Add to these textbook techniques the natural gifts Crane has for swinging in rhythm and imagining different shot shapes and trajectories, and you have one of the best distance wedge games on Tour.

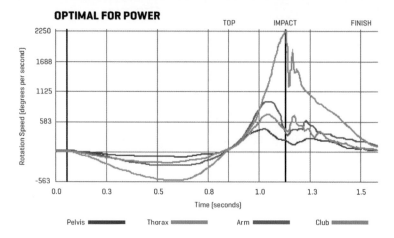

OPTIMAL FOR POWER

HOW TO READ THESE GRAPHS:

The graphs measure rotational speed over time of a player's pelvis, thorax (chest), lead arm, and club as he hits a shot (data provided by the Titleist Performance Institute). The lines that lie below the horizontal axis represent what's happening in the backswing; the lines above this axis represent what's happening in the downswing. The direction of the lines indicates acceleration in terms of rotational velocity. If the line is moving away from the horizontal axis, the element measured is accelerating. If it's moving toward it, the element is decelerating.

In an efficient power sequence (top graph), you can recognize a peaking order of acceleration. The hips (red) accelerate first and then begin to decelerate as the chest (green) begins to rotate and push off the hips. This gives a boost to the chest, which passes the energy on to the arms (blue), which creates a whip or maximum speed of the club (brown) as it strikes the ball.

In stark contrast, the best wedge players use a completely different sequence from ten yards (bottom graph). The club acceleration dominates the start of the downswing, which decelerates the lead arm causing the arm and chest to reverse positions. Through the swing the arms and chest mirror each other reaching maximum velocity after impact, essentially supporting the swinging force of the club. The graph clearly shows that what's optimal for finesse is clearly the opposite of what's optimal for power.

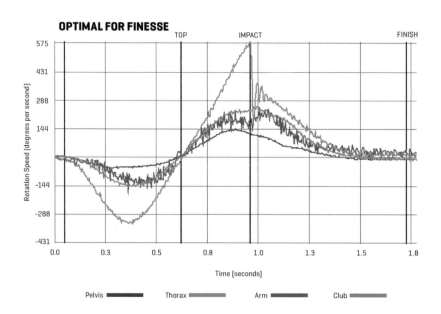

OPTIMAL FOR FINESSE

Use a flatter-faced club such as your 7- or 9-iron (some of my students have gotten really good at putt-chipping with a fairway wood) and grip it like it's your putter. You want as much arm hang as possible, so grip the club down near where the handle meets the steel. Play the ball a tad back of center and lean the shaft two to three degrees toward the target, with the heel section of the club raised slightly off the turf. (The slight camber of the toe area on the sole will help prevent digging through impact). Keep your grip pressure light, but lock in your arms and shoulders. To hit the shot, stay level and swing as though you're stroking a long lag putt.

Your touch on putt-chips (every short-game shot, really) depends on your ability to make the proper length swing in rhythm. Experiment with different clubs to discover your favorite(s), but refrain from using anything with more than 56 degrees of loft. High lofts and extremely shallow swings don't mix.

The Putt-Chip:

STEP 1: Choke all the way down to the steel on a less-lofted iron with the ball a tad back of center. Raise the heel section of the club off the ground.

STEP 2: Using your big muscles, take the club back as though you're hitting a long lag putt.

STEP 3: On your throughswing, stay level, use your big muscles, and maintain a nice rhythm.

STEP 4: Feel as though your arms are "locked in" from start to finish.

2. The Cock-and-Pop

This one is a real "get-out-of-jail-free" shot and is used by all the Tour players I coach. The perfect situation for a cock-and-pop shot is when the ball is buried in thick rough and you have to carry the ball less than 5 yards to a close pin on a firm, fast green, or one that slopes away from you. If the first thing that pops into your head when assessing a lie is "I'm screwed," you should opt for the cock-and-pop.

The cock-and-pop produces an extreme angle of attack, maximum loft, and little power—perfect for the situation described above. It's an odd combination that necessitates extreme adaptations to both your setup and swing. Start by widening your stance and turning both feet out. It should feel as though you're "sitting" a bit. Setting your feet like this aids lower-body stability because it makes it difficult to turn your hips. Lean into your lead thigh and choke down to the bottom of the grip, as you do on other shots that require a steep angle of attack. (Choking down narrows your swing arc, creating a steeper angle as well as reducing the energy of the swing. As Seve used to say, "short shot, short club.") Lastly, create maximum loft by laying the face wide open so that the back of the club lays flat against the turf.

To hit the shot, simply hinge the clubhead straight up using only your wrists—no arm movement, no shoulder movement, and no hip turn. This is the "cock." On your downswing, unhinge or "pop" the clubhead back under the ball using your wrists, with zero hip and chest movement and little or no arm swing. Stay down and hold your weight in your lead thigh all the way to the finish. It'll take some practice to get it right, but it's a lot easier to do than to describe.

The Cock-and-Pop:

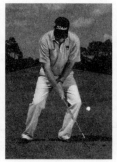

STEP 1: Take an extra-wide stance and sit, holding extra weight in your lead thigh. Lower your hands to near knee-height and lay the face open.

STEP 2: Hinge the club up using only your wrists. This is the "cock."

STEP 3: Throw the clubhead under the ball by unhinging your wrists. This is the "pop."

STEP 4: Everything else stays very quiet. This shot gives you maximum loft and minimal carry.

HOW TO CHOOSE THE APPROPRIATE SHOT

One of the most common questions students ask me is, "How do I know what shot to play?" Being able to see a shot is largely influenced by how you practice, which we'll talk about in the next chapter. One thing that you'll never hear me say is, "Choose the shot that gets the ball rolling on the ground as soon as possible, because this provides a greater margin for error." That's tradition speaking, and it's pure rot! As if it's impossible to skull or chunk a low shot! What if there's a slope in the green you want to avoid, or you're simply better at hitting higher shots than low ones? Shouldn't you play to your strengths? There are simply too many variables that affect shot choice for anyone to try to lobby a universal recommendation. You have to trust your instincts and feel your way through each situation. As far as I'm concerned, the correct shot is the one you see as you walk up to the ball and assess your lie. It's far easier to commit to a shot you see than to one you've been told you *should* play, and it's better to be committed than correct.

Consider the Bounce

Another common question I get is, "How do I play from a tight lie that's into the grain?" The key is in understanding the bounce angle of the club and how you want the club to interact with the turf. Picture a tight lie into the grain that requires a short amount of carry (say, 5 yards) and a waist-high trajectory. You can meet the demands of this shot in three ways: 1) playing a lower-than-normal-trajectory shot with a lob wedge; 2) playing a normal-trajectory shot with a sand wedge; or 3) playing a higher-than-normal-trajectory shot with a pitching wedge (see illustration, page 84). While the effective loft of all three shots may be the same and produce similar ball flights, the effective bounce angles of the three clubs are completely different. When you adjust your setup to play the lower than normal shot with a lob wedge, you're in essence sharpening the leading edge of the club and reducing the bounce, practically ensuring that the club will stick into the grain. This is uncomfortable, and anything but perfect contact will result in a chunk. Taking your pitching wedge and adjusting your setup by removing shaft lean and rotating the clubface open to pull off the higher-trajectory shot lifts the leading edge off the ground and *adds* bounce. Even if you hit a millimeter behind the ball, the club won't dig at all and you'll still enjoy a pretty good outcome.

The lesson: On tight lies into the grain, select a less-lofted club and then adapt your setup to produce a higher-than-normal-trajectory shot.

Shot Selection Effect on Bounce

Situation: Tight Lie into the Grain

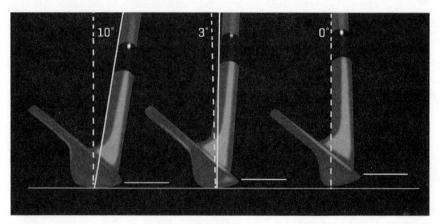

LOB WEDGE
Lower than Normal
Trajectory
10 degrees of shaft lean
NO! Sharp leading edge
with little effective
bounce

SAND WEDGE
Normal Trajectory
3 degrees of shaft lean
OK! Significantly softer
leading edge and more
effective bounce

PITCHING WEDGE
Higher than Normal
Trajectory
0 degrees of shaft lean
YES! Leading edge lifted
off the ground, exposing
maximum amount of
effective bounce.

Obviously, there are a lot of possible situations and setup/swing adaptations to handle them, which is what makes discovering the nuances of the short game so challenging and fun. But how do you get a feel for it all? What you'll find is that experience is the best teacher. I've dedicated my entire adult life to learning and coaching the short game, and I've enjoyed the good fortune of consistently being around the best players in the world. Over time, I've just figured it out. When I work on Tour with someone as talented as Charley Hoffman or Ben Crane, we usually invest only about ten minutes of a two-hour session on technique, because once you understand the finesse wedge principle, the basic shots are easy. What do we do the rest of the time? We scatter balls in every conceivable lie condition and we talk through the shots and adaptations. Being able to see a shot, judge your lie, and know how to adjust is the "art of golf." Use the tricks presented in this chapter to shorten the learning process. Beyond that, however, there are no shortcuts. You have to get out to the practice facility and do a lot of "art."

The good news is that once you learn something about a certain lie, it'll help you the rest of your career, but only if you remember what to do the next time. Write what you learn in your journal. Again, keep it simple and use words and phrases that make sense to you, such as "on downhill lies, think 'fade' swing." Every one of my Tour players makes it a habit to keep notes on the little things they learn. They build into big successes.

CHAPTER 7

WORLD-CLASS WEDGE TRAINING

If you chase short-term results, you'll often feel lost in your pursuit of a better wedge game. Developing the necessary skills demands working in a specific way and experiencing certain things, both of which cannot be circumvented.

One of the first lessons I teach a new student is that what you do today doesn't affect what happens tomorrow—it affects what takes place a month from now. It's a comment on the importance of maintaining a long-term perspective when you train, and on the discipline required to stay on point and allow the cumulative effect of your efforts to work their magic. The Danish-American photographer and social reformer Jacob Riis said it best: "When nothing seems to help, I go look at a stonecutter hammering away at his rock perhaps a hundred times without as much as a crack showing in it. Yet at the hundred and first blow it will split in two, and I know it was not that blow that did it, but all that had gone before."

Improvement isn't an epiphany. It's a *process*, but what does the process for developing a world-class wedge game look like? Obviously, it includes a technical component, a skill-development component and a mental/championship-feeling component. But how much effort do you need to expend? From my own experiences as a struggling mini-tour player, I know that simply "putting in the hours" isn't the answer, and that doing so can actually make you worse. Effective training is about adopting a smart approach to improvement and getting the most out of the time you do invest. At the competitive level, *everyone* practices. Those who train correctly are the ones who reap the greatest benefit.

So let's add two more components to your training. The first is an intensity component. When you practice, it's critical to lock in on your intent at every moment. Working with such high intensity and focus requires significant mental energy, so you can't do it well for a very long period of time. This means you need to practice less than you think. The second extra component is a structural one. There are two goals to training: 1) to confirm that you're executing wedge fundamentals correctly, and 2) to enhance your physical and mental skills. As the intent of what you're trying to accomplish changes (from confirmation to enhancement, and vice versa), so should the structure of the time being invested.

THE RIGHT STUFF

Most golfers don't consider the need for balance in training. They typically spend too much time on one side of the spectrum or the other. Those who dwell too much on skill enhancement are so-called "feel players," which in my book is code for "I don't have a clue what to do and it's too hard to pay attention to fundamental details, so I'll just ignore them completely." (I understand the rationalization, but not the label—everyone plays by feel. That's what golf is.) At the other end of the spectrum are the "technicians," or players who have fallen overly in love with mechanics. These golfers believe that having perfect technique solves every problem. ("If I could just get my right arm in the correct position, I'd be scratch.") They train like robots chasing their own elusive picture of perfection, which changes so often that they fail to reach any destination at all. By failing to balance their work on fundamentals with skill development (the "art" of playing golf), technicians tend to hit the proverbial performance wall.

Personality plays a role for sure, but neither approach on its own can optimize and sustain performance. Great wedge play is science *and* art. Having perfect mechanics means nothing without the ability to feel shots, adjust to varying conditions, or play with confidence. Likewise, the ability to focus on the target and see your shot will take you only so far if your mechanics aren't worthy of your trust. You need both sound fundamentals and the ability to feel the shot and target to be great, and this mandates a structural mix in the type of work you do. LPGA Tour legend and ten-time major winner Annika Sörenstam got it right when she said that one of the reasons she succeeded where others failed was that she "always paid attention to her intention" when she practiced.

BENEFITS AND DRAWBACKS OF BLOCK PRACTICE

When your intent is to work on your fundamentals, you'll benefit more by performing what coaches call "block practice." In block practice, it's critical to put yourself in a pure learning environment—in other words, whatever you're working on must be repeatable, and there must be an available mechanism to confirm that you're doing it correctly. Working on getting the club to move up the shaft plane in your backswing while standing next to a mirror is a great example of block practice. The benefit of block practice isn't solely about learning "how to do it," as most technicians believe. The fact that you're confirming that you are "doing it" is the important part. Learning a new move may take hundreds of repetitions to get right; confirming it may require only five or six. After the initial learning phase (which shouldn't last much longer than a few weeks), you should transition to short bursts of block practice (daily bursts for tournament-level players) while applying forethought and focus to make it pay off.

If block practice is essential, why isn't more of it better? According to an article by Dr. Noa Kageyama in his *Bulletproof Musician* blog on the contextual interference research by Manhattan School of Music professor Dr. Christine Carter, repeatedly doing the same thing over and over is not in line with how our brains work:

> *We are hardwired to pay attention to change, not repetition. This hardwiring can already be observed in proverbial infants. Show a baby the same object over and over again and they'll gradually stop paying attention through a process called "habitization." Change the object and the attention returns full force. The same goes for adults. Functional magnetic resonance imaging has demonstrated that there's progressively less brain activation when stimuli are repeated. The fact is, the repeated information does not receive the same amount of processing as new information.*

We get lured into doing block practice—performing the same act over and over—partly because of our inherent impatience with the learning process and our wanting to feel like we're performing better "right now." We also succumb to block practice because it's easy and makes us feel good. Who wouldn't perform an act better or more comfortably after twenty repetitions? According to Dr. Kageyama, "It's precisely this feeling of comfort and improvement that reinforces our reliance on block practice. The problem with this kind of practicing, however, is that the positive results we feel in the practice room today do not lead to the best long-term learning tomorrow."

Block practice breeds both a false sense of competency and false confidence, which quickly disappears when we face the realities of our on-course performance later on. Moreover, the technician's belief that they'll ultimately reach technique perfection has been proven by science to be a futile one, because our brains are wired for adaptability, not consistency. To wit, research performed on the neural basis of sensorimotor integration and movement control by Stanford University professors Dr. Krishna Shenoy, Dr. Mark Churchland, and Dr. Afsheen Afshar:

Our brains simply do not allow us to "code" the swing perfectly so it will repeat time after time. We are all in a sense doomed to a level of inconsistent swings. It's as if each time the brain tries to solve the problem of planning how to move, it does it anew. Practice and training can help the brain solve the problem more capably, but people and other primates simply aren't wired for consistency, like computers or machines. Instead, people seem to be improvisers by default.

One of the beautiful things in golf is that no two shots are alike. Being able to adapt, trust, and judge are of the utmost value, and there's less time available to develop these essential skills when you waste time trying to perfect the "unperfectable." Again, the Stanford professors:

Most players, when performing poorly, attribute the result to technique and spend more time practicing. Yet, the survey results show that players who are "on track" are actually practicing less! The pervasive belief is we can "groove" our swing to the point it just repeats and repeats while science is telling us the brain will never allow this to happen. If we accept the fact that the swing will always be somewhat variable from day to day, then practice can take on a more constructive approach. The message: flexibility beats consistency.

Science clearly supports my observational belief that overdoing block practice carries with it diminishing returns. So why do it at all? As both a coach and a player, I know that a golfer's life is a petri dish for the ongoing experiment of "feel versus real," which is one of the reasons why golf is both the best game to play and the most difficult. Usually, when you start playing poorly, it's only because you're not doing what you think you are. Sure, you can define and write down the fundamentals that you believe in (chest pointed in front of the ball, club up the plane with the toe up, finesse sequence, etc.), but are you actually executing them? You can't assume either yes or no. A reasonable number of perfect repetitions in a well-designed daily block-practice session will provide

Block practice with PGA Tour player Nick Watney prior to the 2011 Honda Classic. When we are doing block practice, we work on one fundamental at a time, with the focus and intensity needed to make sure we are doing it exactly right.

the confirmation you need and keep you heading down the correct path. Continuity will ultimately breed confidence and mastery. As I say to my students, "A little bit of well-designed block practice a day keeps the swing doctor away."

BENEFITS AND DRAWBACKS OF RANDOM PRACTICE

When your intent shifts from fundamentals to enhancing your physical and mental skills, block practice takes a backseat. Here, the most efficient way to work is through "random practice." As you progress through my wedge systems, random training will make up approximately 70 percent of your practice-time investment. Why? Because there's so much beyond executing technique. Great players are great judges, and nothing improves judgment like randomly assessing shots. Things like choosing the right club and shot for the situation you're facing; landing the ball in the appropriate spot; controlling trajectory; sensing grain, wind, and break; imparting the correct amount of energy to the ball; and adapting to varied lies so that you can strike the ball solidly regardless of the circumstance. Random practice is an opportunity to practice being mentally organized so that you can maintain focus, build confidence, and adopt a resilient attitude regardless of outcome, traits that all represent the mind and judgment skills of a champion. It's what made Seve Ballesteros a legend. Random practice is nothing more than using focus and attention to learn something from every swing, and then tapping this knowledge to further refine the ability in question. I call this doing "hard math," and I commonly give the following example in my golf schools:

Two aspiring students stage a math competition. One student performs the same basic problem over and over $(7 + 7, 7 + 7, 7 + 7,$ etc.$)$. The other completes half as many problems, but attempts more difficult and varied equations $(108 + 71, 146 - 33, 66 \times 3,$ etc.$)$. The competition lasts a month. It's easy to tell which student, after thirty days, will have worked harder and is destined to become the better mathematician.

Even though your daily performances may feel worse when you're doing random-practice sessions, these skills will transfer to the course more effectively than the ones developed under block-practice conditions.

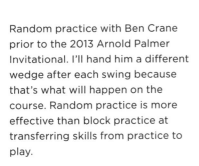

Random practice with Ben Crane prior to the 2013 Arnold Palmer Invitational. I'll hand him a different wedge after each swing because that's what will happen on the course. Random practice is more effective than block practice at transferring skills from practice to play.

Improving Your Intentions

It doesn't matter how or what you're practicing—you always have to be focused and purposeful. This is the "intensity" component to effective training. Typically, I reserve 10 to 20 percent of my practice time for playing games. Anytime you're forced to post a score with a reward or punishment that goes along with the outcome (i.e., a game), your intensity and focus skyrockets. Everyone wants to win, so games naturally get you out of doing the things that typically lead to ineffective practice, like being complacent or "going through the motions." Games elevate skill transfer. If you succeed on the practice facility, you'll succeed on the course. Many times I ask my players to "win" their way off the green (or out of the bunker) through a game. It's the perfect way to end a training session.

YOUR BALANCED FOCUSED PRACTICE PLAN

BLOCK PRACTICE: FUNDAMENTAL DEVELOPMENT
10 to 20 percent of your daily dedicated practice time

1. Pay attention to your intention. What are you going to accomplish in this time frame?
2. Pay attention to the details: grip, alignment, ball position, balance, etc.
3. Put yourself in a learning environment: Go slow; focus internally; practice with immediate, accurate, and reliable feedback.
4. Be honest with yourself. Occasionally take inventory and adjust your plan if necessary (using video or by taking a lesson).
5. When making changes, focus on the process and not the immediate results.
6. Stay focused on the same thought for at least three weeks.
7. When training mechanics, intersperse drills with regular swings. (Remember, it won't always be fun or comfortable when changing to a new move.)
8. Never practice "looking" at a target while "thinking" mechanics. Hit into open space or remove the ball from the equation when possible. Once you have the confirmation you need, quit.

RANDOM PRACTICE: SKILL DEVELOPMENT
70 percent of your daily dedicated practice time

1. Practice your full process and "trusting" with external focus (see page 102). Picture yourself in tournament situations; take the time to get focused on the target and the shot.

2. Shape shots: high, low, draws, fades, etc. Take five yards off or add five yards to your stock shot.
3. Change clubs, lies (uphill, downhill, rough, etc.) and targets frequently.
4. Practice every part of the game and every conceivable situation.
5. Run your full championship-feeling program, including post-shot error detection and positive imprinting (see page 104).
6. The goal of this type of practice is to learn to perform the action subconsciously and do it without thinking, as you do when you're tying your shoelaces.

GAMES: TRANSFER TRAINING
10 to 20 percent of your daily dedicated practice time

1. Win your way off the practice facility by playing a simple game, like "Three In a Row": Hit three fades, draws, or any kind of shot in a row to a certain standard before rewarding yourself with lunch or dinner. (More games listed starting on page 109.) The ability to produce three in a row in practice will translate into the ability to execute that shot with confidence on the course when it counts.
2. Compete against set goals (as in the game "21") or other like-minded individuals.

This is the right formula to work both "hard and smart" and develop a competitive advantage. Stick to it. If you only have thirty minutes to practice one day, spend only three to five minutes on block training to make sure that your fundamentals are sound. I liken this to Stephen Covey's analogy in *The 7 Habits of Highly Effective People*: "Let's make sure that the saw is sharp before we wade into the forest and cut the trees down." Once your saw is sharp (i.e., block practice is complete), transition to random practice. Work on your process (the steps you run through to get ready to play a shot) as well as your judgment skills and ability to attain and maintain focus. Don't get stuck in a spot, and never allow yourself a do-over. Rehearse the solution or correction in your mind, then move on. Practice being resilient and tough. Learn, put it behind you, and refocus on the next shot.

After fifteen minutes or so of random practice, finish your training session by winning your way off the practice facility playing one of the practice games presented in Chapter 9 (my favorite is 21).

Practicing within this structure produces maximum efficiency and maximum benefit for the time invested. It should be flexible, because some days you'll be able to train longer than others. Despite structure, your plan shouldn't be so regimented that it stifles you.

Regardless of how often or for how long you practice, perform your block-practice exercises every time. This may sound like I'm contradicting the research, but I believe that having a well-designed block-practice regimen is the key to keeping you on track long enough so you can own what you do and remove doubt when you play. It takes so little time, and the mental benefit of knowing you have a "sharp saw" is too important to neglect. I also want you to win your way off the practice facility without fail. If designed properly, a game also takes very little time to play and fosters the desire to compete, which is something all great players relish.

Be adaptive to the day by adjusting how long you spend in random-practice mode. On days when you have a lot of time, do as much random practice as you want, or as long as your intensity and focus remain high. When your time is limited, eliminate random practice completely, especially if you're playing golf that day. The act of playing is in itself random training, but don't ever confuse "warming up" with "practice." When you're warming up, you're trying to get your body and mind ready to compete. When you're practicing, you're trying to confirm a fundamental technique or grow a skill. These sessions shouldn't feel or look remotely similar.

Real practice—the kind that'll actually make a difference—takes knowledge about what to do, forethought about how to do it, feedback while you're doing it, a willingness to be uncomfortable, and mental discipline and focus. Real practice is tiring, which is why very few people actually do it. Will you? I would hope that your desire or passion for growth, and the knowledge that high-level performers have always separated themselves from others of equal talent by the type of work they do, will keep you on point. The fun you have as you grow and play up to or near your athletic potential will be all the reward you need.

CHAPTER 8

WEDGING IT WITH THE MIND OF A CHAMPION

In the mind of a championship competitor, emotion comes first.

G reat wedge players compete with what I call a "championship feeling." You've heard of "playing like a champion" or "thinking like a champion," but this is something different. I use the term "feeling" because when it comes to being mentally strong, emotions (i.e., your feelings) come first, and if they're not up to championship level, they'll end up *owning* you instead of the other way around. You can't play like a champion until you learn to think like one, and you can't think like a champion until you feel like one.

Case in point? Me, the struggling mini-tour player of the late 1980s and mid-1990s. I remember how the worse I played, the harder I worked—and the more brain-dead I became. Actually, it was just the opposite: I thought way too much—bad stuff—and despite knowing better, I couldn't turn my brain off or stop it from running negative highlight reels in my head. I tried reading books on sports psychology and listening to tapes, but nothing worked. The information was good, but my mind wasn't in a place to receive it. For example, if someone instructed me to "visualize the shot," I'd visualize the ball kicking into a bunker, sliding out of bounds, or lipping out. I had spent too many years "beating myself down" instead of building myself up.

CONTROLLING EMOTIONS

At the 2008 Honda Classic, I saw a new face working with my longtime student Charlie Wi and, later on, three-time major winner Vijay Singh. I hadn't met Dr. Bruce Wilson before or knew much about him, but after researching who he was and his involvement with the revolutionary Heart Math method (heartmath.org) for controlling emotions, I hired him on the spot to teach me as much as he could.

For years at his medical practice in Milwaukee, Dr. Wilson witnessed people who could not deal with stressful situations and saw how it led to cardiovascular disease. He taught me how emotions affect physical health, athletic performance, and quality of life, and how the ultimate performance state is one of high-energy, positive emotion. Through his guidance, I began to recognize the destructive mental patterns I had experienced on Tour. Rarely did I play in a high-energy, positive-emotion state (i.e., excited, happy, having fun yet determined). I toiled in either high- or low-energy, negative-emotion states (i.e., fearful, anxious, angry, and helpless). Other times, I completely tuned out my feelings, in the mistaken belief that showing any emotion was a sign of weakness.

It was time to undo the damage. I began to explore strategies to change those emotions and to channel my negative energy toward something more productive. I started to realize just how important a post-shot routine (the things you do after you swing) is to maintaining a positive vibe during practice and play, and I began teaching these techniques to my students. It made a huge

Are you managing your emotions or are your emotions managing you?

difference in their games, not to mention to me personally. The mental game is an essential part of every one of my coaching sessions—it's just too big a piece of the performance pie to ignore.

"See" Yourself as the Player You Want to Be

At Ben Crane's year-end team meeting following the conclusion of the 2010 season, I was introduced to his mental-game coach, Lanny Bassham. Crane had raved about him all year: He was a world-class rifle shooter with multiple Olympic medals and world records who had become one of the top performance experts in the business. As Bassham reiterated his philosophies at the team meeting and explained what he expected from Ben in 2011 from a "Mental Management" (Lanny's trademark term) perspective, I wanted to stand up and applaud. The beliefs I had developed about the mental game since working with Dr. Wilson almost three years earlier finally had a voice.

Bassham spoke a lot about self-image, or how Crane viewed himself in relation to the activity he was performing. "Ben," he asked, "when you walk up with a wedge in your hand to a tough finesse shot over a bunker, if you could look in a mirror right then, what would you see?" This is a make-or-break question when it comes to performance, because the mirror will reflect an image of either emotional health or damage. Moreover, the image changes with the situation. You may have a high self-image with a driver in your hand, but a low one with a wedge. Your self-image is probably higher on your home course during a round with your buddies than it is when playing in a member-guest on a course you don't know.

The fact that your self-image (what Bassham calls "S.I.") changes in different environments means that it can be controlled. You're not stuck with the same S.I., like you are with your eye color or height. If I pay you a compliment after you hit a great shot, your S.I. grows. With a higher S.I., you'll start to walk with a swagger, feel like time is slowing down for you and execute fluid shots. Perfect. Unfortunately, it works the other way, too, and your coach won't always be there to prop you up. This puts you in charge of your S.I., and unfortunately, from what I've seen, most weekend players fail to manage it. The self-deprecation is amazing: "That was horrible," "I stink," and "I'll never be any good if I hit shots like that." Giving your S.I. a beating like this makes subsequent shots seem harder, which in turn makes you anxious. And the more anxious you are, the more your mind will race. The game will speed up and you'll have difficulty maintaining focus and fluidity. At this point, technique and conscious thought no longer matter—your feelings are driving your poor shotmaking. Basically, you're spiraling out of control and becoming your own worst enemy.

My experiences with Dr. Wilson and Lanny Bassham have taught me that feeling like a champion is dependent on your ability to protect and grow your S.I. on a daily basis. This is the first step toward becoming a strong mental competitor. I teach four strategies to help make it happen.

1. Develop a *Post-Shot* Routine

How you react and evaluate yourself immediately after you hit a shot is critical if you're going to feel like a champion and play up to your potential, because this is when your S.I. is most conducive to change. If you think about it, only one of two things can happen after a swing: an outcome that makes you happy or one that doesn't. Here's how to deal with both.

When You Hit a Good Shot . . .

. . . immediately take a moment and internalize it; take ownership with some emotion attached, and imbed it in your mind. Say, "Yes, that's the real me." Doing this creates positive emotions and increases confidence. It sounds simplistic, but most golfers never give themselves credit for hitting good shots. They stiff a shot from 170 yards and act like it was supposed to happen, as if pulling off a successful shot is always a forgone conclusion (which it isn't)! Watch Tiger Woods or any elite player react to a great shot. They twirl the club, pump their fist, flash a smile—they get fired up! Emotion cements memory, and most of us only display it after bad shots, which of course is counterproductive.

When You Hit a Bad Shot . . .

. . . immediately objectify it. Keep your emotions in check and literally state a solution. Think, "If I had a do-over, what would I do differently?" The solutions are endless (a different club or target, higher commitment level to the shot, more hip turn, etc.) and vary for every shot and every player. This is where the true role of a coach comes in. A good coach should be able to help his or her player understand their misses with absolute certainty, then provide simple solutions. When I hit a weak flare to the right, I know that my upper body tilted back in the downswing and I carried the handle, so the solution for me is to stay level as I rotate. When I chunk a finesse shot, or fly it farther than I intend to, I know that my tempo in the transition was quick, which ruined the sequence. My solution is to maintain a lighter grip pressure and feel as though the club is doing all of the work. Because I know what my misses mean when they happen, I can immediately play the swing over in my mind the correct way and recommit to my fundamentals. And even though I hit a poor shot, I end up being even more committed to my fundamentals and sure of myself. I control my emotional state so that it can't control or limit me. The immature or undisciplined can't imagine this possibility. With this approach, every shot has the opportunity to make you a better player, regardless of its outcome. Your good shots are confidence-builders, and your bad ones are learning opportunities. There's nothing but winning and learning when you have a championship mentality.

The facts are simple: humans learn by making mistakes, processing information, and adapting based on their knowledge and experience so that they can avoid repeating them. A baby falls hundreds of times before he learns to walk. Would he learn to walk faster or better if every time he fell he told himself how pathetic he was? The great U.C.L.A. basketball coach John Wooden once said, "Why do we dread adversity when we know that facing it is the only way to become stronger, smarter, and better?"

Completing Your Routine

The last step of a quality post-shot routine, and perhaps the most important, is "letting go." Once you've mentally corrected a bad shot, be done with it. Don't take the negative experience of the last shot to the next one. Don't take it to the next hole. And for sure, don't take it home. Negativity stifles the learning process and makes peak performance impossible. It's like carrying around a ton of bricks; it tires the body and burdens the mind. Is that what golf is supposed to be like? No! Golf is a journey that should be filled with joy! Regardless of what happens, each round has the potential to be a great one.

2. Count Your Blessings

One of the strategies Dr. Wilson suggested to me was to start an "appreciation journal." I'm 100 percent certain that everyone, regardless of who they are and what's happening in their life, has many things to feel blessed about. It's more a matter of whether you choose to recognize and focus on them or not.

On the computer you use daily, or in your short game journal, create a document (or page) and title it "My Blessings." Invest two minutes per day, every day, to feel the strong positive emotion of counting your blessings. Do it the first thing in the morning, or as you have your coffee. Don't wait until after you check your e-mail or start returning texts and phone calls or any activity that may distract or derail you. Write down one thing that you're either thankful for or recognize as a blessing. Keep it to one sentence, and don't make it difficult. It can be anything as long as it's true. Here are the first five entries I made in my appreciation journal, started more than five years ago:

- I appreciate having a job where I can easily see God's beauty and breathe in oxygen-rich air.
- I appreciate the convenience and possibilities that modern transportation lends.
- I am thankful for the support of my wife, my family, and my friends.
- I love the fact that I can enjoy and savor the flavor of so many foods (steak, pasta, wine, etc.).
- It makes me happy that the dogs greet me at the door so joyfully when I come home.

After a while the blessings will start to accumulate, and you'll marvel at just how good things really are. Before you put away your journal, randomly pick and reflect on two previous entries. It takes two minutes to write down one blessing and reflect on two others—a very quick way to get your day started off on an emotionally positive note. Having the right perspective and attitude is a habit. So is winning. Win those first two minutes and you just may win the day.

3. Dare to Dream

You can't control your dreams when you're asleep, but you can when you're awake. Use them to build an image of how you'd like your round to go with the intent of imbedding the acts you want to take place into your subconscious. Get comfortable in a nice quiet place and start taking slow, deep breaths: Inhale for four seconds, exhale for four seconds. As you focus on your breathing, let your muscles relax and your mind clear. Now, imagine yourself as you want to be when you show up to the course. *You're confident and unhurried as you walk through the parking lot to the clubhouse, your belief in yourself growing with each step.* Go through a typical warm-up. *You're graceful and relaxed as you hit a few drivers, a few putts and some short-game shots.* See your swings in slow motion and mentally feel their motion right where you sit. Go through your pre-shot routine. *You're walking into each shot clear and committed to your strategy.* Recall previous great moments on the course. *That's how I'm going to feel today when I play.* See yourself knocking in a putt on the last hole and feel satisfaction with the result.

Your dream exercise is complete. Repeat it every day. It takes but ten minutes. Remember, the type of work that you do and your approach to improvement has as much or more to do with greatness than talent.

4. Gain Perspective

Golf is what you do, not who you are. When you play poorly, you're no less the human being than when you play great. There's you and then there's your score, and never the twain shall meet. To make sure the number on your card doesn't swallow you up (or put your nose in the air), find something outside the game to put energy into and draw satisfaction from: your church, your family, your physical fitness, etc. Make it something positive. I call this "having a glass of perspective." (Those of you old enough to have an adult beverage know what I'm talking about.) Sometimes we make the little things more important than they are and lose sight of the big picture. With the right perspective, a bad shot or poor performance will have no effect on your S.I., or deter you from the vision of what you plan to accomplish.

CHAMPIONSHIP THINKING STRATEGIES

You now have three strategies and a mindset to feel like a champion. With your emotions under control, you can now start *thinking* like a champion. Like anything else, it comes down to the choices you make. As humans, we have volition, the power to choose our thoughts and actions. Volition—not prudence—allows us to climb Mount Everest, win medals of honor in battle, and create fine art. How we think and what we do are choices. Here are nine areas of mental performance that'll either make or break you, depending on the route you follow.

1. Choose Mental Toughness: Make decisions with conviction and a commitment to "this is how it's gonna be today!" Picture a swimming pool—in *January*. Even though the water is freezing, you think it's a good day for a swim and test the water with your big toe. The rush of cold from the water, however, suddenly creates uncertainty and weakens your resolve. Now you have second thoughts. But what if you made the conscious decision to walk to the edge of the pool and jump in as soon as you reached its edge, freezing water be damned? That's commitment. That's the power of volition. The more committed you are to your decision, the more control you have over what's going to happen (jump in the cold pool, finish that proposal at work, hit wedge shots without fear, etc.), and the easier it'll be to do it.

2. Separate Internal and External Focus: As you read the guidelines for effective training in the last chapter, you likely noticed the terms "internal" and "external" focus. These refer to where your thoughts reside and what you're focused on. If your thoughts are internally focused, you're thinking about specific movements within your body during the swing, such as keeping your head still. Internal focus is essential only during block practice. That's when the little details matter as you work toward mastery. This is how you learn, not how you play. Internal focus can be a drug, and those that become addicted to it lose feel for the game and rarely have those rounds where everything falls easily into place. Great golf—great shotmaking—requires external focus, which resides outside the confines of your body and club. Focusing externally allows an action to occur automatically or subconsciously, like when you tied your shoelaces this morning. There's no "how" when you're externally focused, there's just "do."

Most players, however, go to the range for an hour, thinking internally about mechanics for the entire sixty minutes, then head to the course somehow expecting to see the shot and "let it go." Since your habits are defined by what you do most of the time, it's not going to happen this way. This is one reason why I'm so particular about the type of work I ask my students to do. You have to take the time to ensure that your fundamentals are in order (internal focus, block practice) before you can trust them, which requires its own type of training (external focus, random practice). The proper practice mix is built into the training programs outlined in this book, but it's important that you're aware of its ingredients. Remember, your intent dictates your focus.

With this in mind, I have two additional guidelines for practice and performance. First, I believe it's impossible to focus on the target and your movement at the same time. That's why I ask my players to remove the target during block practice and hit into open space, which allows them to focus and evaluate solely on movement and not outcome. When it comes to random practice time, I reintroduce the pin. A clear target essentially becomes a cue to think about only what you want the ball to do using external focus and positive images.

Second, manage your thoughts. Imagination and feel are right-brain activities that require mental clarity and focus. Your conscious mind can only hold one thought at a time, so if you're thinking about your technique, you're failing to engage or react to the target—the ultimate goal. This doesn't eliminate the usefulness of swing thoughts, however. A single swing key can buoy confidence and be a catalyst to great execution. Where it resides in your mind is the critical factor. Is it something you're simply aware of, or is it a predominant thought or a command on how to play? Commands tend to ruin athletic motion and timing, while a simple awareness of a mechanic (if subservient to a strong focus on the shot) doesn't. Understanding this dynamic can make a huge difference in your mental game and on-course performance.

3. Choose to Prioritize "Quality Position": Quality position refers to your ability to keep the ball in the right area of the course relative to the pin so that you leave yourself easy shots. Whether it's creating an open angle when hitting into the green so that you don't have to carry a hazard, or leaving yourself an easy finesse wedge or putt, maintaining quality position is one of the most important ingredients of good scoring. I know a lot of amateurs who can reel off four or five pars in a row without blinking but fail to break 80, because they make several double- or triple-bogeys each round. The ball won't always go where you want it to, but if you identify the quality position before you select each shot, and strategize as if a Tour caddy is on your bag, I bet you'd cut the amount of times you leave yourself an impossible short-game shot in half. Easy shots lead to low scores. Hard shots lead to the occasional train wreck.

4. Master Your Process: When I talk about process, I'm referring to the steps you run through, both physically and mentally, that optimize your chances for success and long-term growth before you even hit the shot. It encompasses your pre-shot routine, the shot itself and the post-shot routine. The goal of your pre-shot routine is to narrow your focus so you can clearly commit and react to what you see. Picture a funnel. At the top is where you pour in all of the information you've gathered about the shot you're facing: the wind, yardage, lie, slope, etc. As this data moves through the funnel, things get narrower and clearer until a strategy is formulated. As it nears the bottom, you start to visualize the shot and feel the movement necessary to produce it. Ultimately, you end up with a precise output that allows you to react without conscious thought or effort; an automated response to your vision. All that's left to do is calmly pull the trigger with a clear committed mind. The illustration on the next page shows the funnel-like process for a 10-yard finesse wedge shot.

Your shot is either going to be good or bad—intended or unintended. After a good shot, take ownership emotionally—imprint. After your poor ones, choose to be solution-oriented and learn something. Make and replay the correction and then be done—move on.

The Process

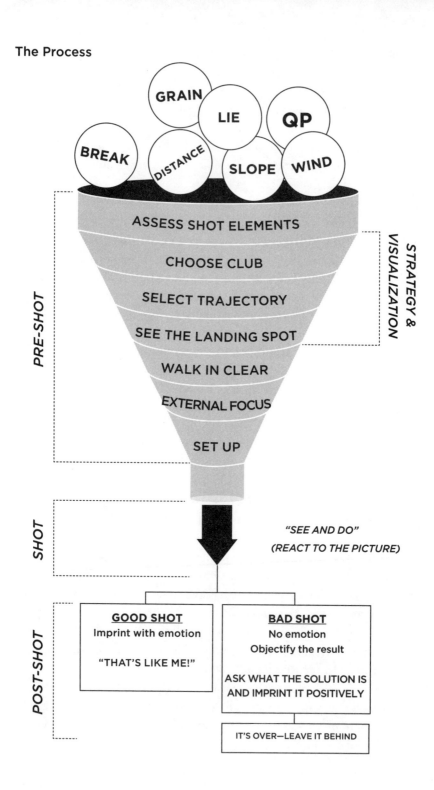

5. Choose to Make Process the Most Important Thing: Champions often choose to make the process more important than the outcome. The reason this is a championship mindset is that it's easy to control the process of a shot but not always possible to control its results. I've hit plenty of great-looking and great-feeling shots in my day that flew the green, plugged under the lip of a bunker, or took a wicked kick into shrubs. It's counterproductive and draining to worry about things outside your control, which are numerous in golf: wind, temperature, course conditions, annoying playing partners, misjudgment, and your standing to par or other players.

Only think about and evaluate things you can control. If you executed a solid process and the shot felt like you imagined it would feel, it deserves high marks regardless of the outcome. Sometimes this is difficult to accept, but you have to make it a way of life. I know several PGA Tour players who evaluate and "score" their process for each shot and each round and let the chips fall where they may. I suggest you create a process score when you play and practice and work on improving it daily. When the process becomes the thing you care about the most and evaluate the hardest, you're free from expectation and liberated to simply play the game.

Your new mantra is: "I'm not overly concerned by the result of any shot, because I'm not a robot and hitting both good and bad shots is a natural part of the game. I know that being a champion takes faith and resiliency. I have faith

Expert at Work!

Watch me run through my full process for hitting a successful finesse wedge shot on a special video. Visit jsegolfacademy.com/index.php/james-sieckmann.

because my fundamentals are good, and I'm working hard on doing the right things the right way. In the long run, the results will take care of themselves and I will achieve my goals."

6. Set Process Goals: Setting goals is clearly valuable. In Chapter 3, I asked you to come up with some performance goals ("I will shoot in the 70s") and write them in your journal. Now I'd like you to set a few process goals. A process goal deals with the little things you can control today that'll add up to something bigger in the end. Here are some quality examples:

- To have the most effective, most disciplined post-shot routine at the club, in the tournament, in my state, etc.
- To win with attitude. (I borrowed this from student and PGA Tour player Cameron Tringale.)
- To walk into every shot with clear commitment, thinking only about what I want in a positive way.
- To practice harder and smarter than anyone I know.

7. Invest In the Future (but Live in the Present): Helplessness, anger, and frustration are emotions tied to the past. Fear and anxiety live in the future, along with outcome. Ignore both and commit to playing in the present. Perform one task at a time, one shot at a time, and one step in your process at a time.

8. Try Just the Right Amount: Can you "over-try" in golf? Of course you can! Doing so, however, creates tension, which ruins timing and fluidity and makes it more challenging to be resilient when things don't go according to plan. Develop an awareness of your "try" level and set yours to "just hard enough" all day. To me, "just hard enough" lives somewhere between "let's just have fun out there today" and "look and play fearlessly today."

9. Be OK: There's a famous mental-game story on Tour about a father-son duo that any golfer can learn from. (The father is a famous coach, and the son would go on to become a major champion, but I won't name names.) As the boy became a teenager and started competing on a national level, the father took him out one day to a particularly difficult driving hole and instructed him to tee up a ball and hit it into the lake left of the fairway. The son gave his father a quizzical look, but did as instructed. The father then asked his son to tee up a second ball and hit it into the houses beyond the course's boundary to the right. After launching the ball O.B. and into the neighboring homes, the father asked, "Are you OK?" The son answered, "Yes, I'm fine." "All right," the father replied, "now tee up another ball and hit it down the fairway."

The message is simple and clear: Regardless of what happens to your ball, it's just a shot. It can't really cause harm unless you let it. Don't allow yourself to be defined by your results. In big moments, you have to be willing to lose—and be OK with it—in order to win. This takes maturity, a healthy S.I., and perspective.

As Shakespeare wrote, "There is nothing either good or bad, but thinking makes it so."

JOURNAL WORK

○ Go to the championship-feeling section of your journal and start the proactive process of becoming the player you want to be. Write down the four strategies to control emotion and grow and protect your S.I. Define your post-shot routine, start the first day of your blessing journal, and define a suitable time and place every day to dream and see yourself as the person you want to be tomorrow, and to note the instances or circumstances where you commonly lose perspective. Write down an action plan—what you're going to do about each.

○ Next, review my championship-thinking strategies. Be honest with yourself and note which ones, if any, you've been failing at. Once again, getting in touch with your mental-game deficiencies is an important step, but it's the development of an action plan to improve them that'll make the difference. Write down what you're going to do to change your habits.

○ Your mental plan should start coming into focus. Review and amend this section of your journal regularly to keep your plan relevant and up-to-date. Remember, the little things add up to great things.

CHAPTER 9

FINESSE WEDGE TRAINING PLAN

Talent matters, but not as much as the type of work you do.

Armed with the basic structure of an effective finesse wedge training program (including the proper mix of block, random, and game practice), you're ready to establish some specifics. The first step is to piece together a block-practice regimen that matches your fundamental flaws with the drills and fixes presented in Chapter 5. Map out and execute your block-practice drills in the following order: 1) address, 2) backswing, and 3) delivery. As always with block practice, focus intently on what you're trying to accomplish, and complete your work expediently so that you can move on to other facets of performance. Remember, your block training should take up only 10 to 20 percent of your typical daily training time.

As you transition from block practice to random practice and game playing, be sure to switch your focus from internal to external, paying attention to your process and championship-feeling strategies. Your training should encompass a technical component, a skill-development component, and a mental component. This allows you to improve daily and sustain that growth over time. Quality training (intention, focus, and intensity) beats quantity training, so limit any finesse wedge practice session to thirty minutes. Stop as soon as you sense that your focus is waning.

PRACTICE AND ACCOUNTABILITY

The effectiveness of your finesse wedge training program depends on your discipline level. Stay on task and resist the urge to chase short-term outcomes.

Make yourself accountable for your results. Many of the Tour players I coach text me their "21" game scores on a near-weekly basis and record them in their journal. When I receive these texts, I know the player is on point and working hard and smart. Some of them even send me voice memos after every round that detail the things they did well, what they learned during the round, and what they're going to do about it going forward. Many of the players set goals for each area, and we grade how they (we, really) did at the team meeting at the end of the season. Accountability works.

This is another place where keeping a journal will pay huge dividends. In the finesse wedge section of your notebook, make sure you've already noted any flaws in your finesse wedge fundamentals and an appropriate fix or drill to correct the error and change the motor pattern. These exercises are what make up your block-practice sessions. Complete your daily block training by hitting three different trajectory shots with the same club to the same pin as described on page 71. Lower than normal, normal, and higher than normal. It's a great way to build confidence by reminding yourself that you have and can produce any shot you see. Also, it's a way to transition from block practice to random practice, where you're essentially playing golf (using your full process and full routine on every shot). In addition to writing down your plan, leave room in your journal to record the results of the games you play, as well as the things you may have learned that day. Nothing beats learning from your mistakes—write down everything you see and experience and note an action plan for how you're going to respond to it going forward.

The typical finesse wedge training program is neither complicated nor physically demanding. I've said nothing about it "being easy." You'll need to muster as much focus, discipline, and mental effort as possible. It can be done, and when you do it, you'll be miles ahead of your competition. You'll not only sustain improvement, you'll maximize your time and energy investment and, most important, your enjoyment during the journey.

INTENTFUL PRACTICE FINESSE WEDGE GAMES

Play 21

Play nine random short-game holes (three easy, three medium, and three difficult) from 30 yards and in with one ball, and score each hole by the total number of strokes it takes you to hole out. Over the course of the nine holes, be sure to use the full gamut of your wedges.

Step 1: Select a target pin on the short-game practice green, then toss your ball to a random spot (again, within 30 yards of the pin).

Step 2: Play the ball as it lies and finesse it onto the green using your full process.

Step 3: Continue until you hole-out with your putter (or wedge). Choose the next pin and toss the ball into another random spot. Remember to create a mix of easy, medium, and difficult holes.

Step 4: Par for this nine-hole "course" is 21, which could be represented by six up-and-ins and three down-in-threes. A good score is 21 or less for a pro or competitive amateur and 23 for mid-handicaps.

This is my favorite finesse wedge practice game. It allows you to play nine short shots under competitive conditions in about ten minutes. During a normal four-hour round of golf you're afforded only six or so of these short-game opportunities. My Tour students play 21 twice a week on competition weeks and every day on off-weeks. You can also play this game on the course if the opportunity presents itself. Simply toss the ball off the green after you hole out (say, on every other hole) and play it in, keeping a separate score for your "21" round. It's a great way to get the feel for course conditions that you may not be familiar with.

Knockout

Select a pin that's about 10 yards from the edge of the green. Create six same-size landing zones about five feet in length starting from the apron. (Use coins or tees to mark the zones.) Empty a small bucket of balls on a spot anywhere from 1 to 20 yards off the green, making sure each ball is in line with the landing zones and the cup. The goal is to eliminate each zone in order (either front to back or back to front) by landing the ball within its dimensions and controlling club choice and trajectory so that the ball ends up within six feet of the hole.

Example: Choose landing zone 1 (the one closest to your lie). Select the appropriate club and trajectory and execute the shot. If you're successful, then you've eliminated that zone—proceed to the next one. If not, repeat. Knock out each zone in succession. Your knockout score is the total number of balls it takes you to eliminate all six zones. The best score I've ever witnessed is a 10. Set a winning score based on your skill level and use it as a benchmark to gauge improvement. Shooting a personal-best Knockout score will prove both rewarding and effective.

Ten-Ball Make

Select ten random 10-yard short-game shots. Make them pretty simple—so easy that you should think about holing each one out. Play all ten shots with the goal of making a minimum of two. One make or less is a loss, and two or more is a win. This game fosters the correct focus for using your wedge game to make birdies. For comparison, the Tour leader in getting up and down from within 10 yards of the green is around 95 percent.

Throw Darts

Same rules as 21, but in Darts you don't have to hole out. Score each hole based on the proximity to the pin following your first shot using the following scoring system:

Make: 5 points

Inside 1 club length: 3 points
Inside 2 club lengths: 2 points
Inside 3 club lengths: 1 point

Outside 3 club lengths: 0 points

Tournament-level players should achieve a minimum Dart score of eighteen points. Yours may differ based on your skill level. As always, use your score to set goals, track progress, and gun for a personal best.

Leap Frog

From a spot at least 10 yards from the edge of the green and approximately 30 yards from the pin, wedge a ball just barely onto the putting surface. On your next shot, attempt to hit the ball past the first one but keep it on your side of the cup. Hit a third ball past the second and again keep it on your side of the hole. Keep "leap-frogging" this way and see how many balls you can get onto the green in order without going past the pin. You get one mulligan. This game helps you develop touch and distance control and teaches you to become aware of how the ball reacts on the green given the trajectory and lie conditions. Your goal: a personal-best score every time you play.

Six-Up

Challenge a player of similar skill level to a short-game shootout. Player A picks the hole and then randomly throws both balls off the green, producing similar lies and shots. Player A plays first. The goal is to get the ball close, if not in. Use the following scoring system:

> 1 point for closest to the hole
> 3 points for a hole out
> 5 points for holing out on top of your competitor (who gets 0)

Player B chooses the next hole and throws the balls. Same scoring. The game continues in alternating order until one player gets six points ahead of the other, at which point the game is won. Vary the throws to require the use of as many finesse clubs as possible.

This is a fantastic game if you're lucky enough to have a buddy who's good enough to push you and create pressurized moments. My brother and I played it all the time when we were younger, and I've seen players of the caliber of Tom Pernice Jr. and Charley Hoffman go at it for hours. You'll be surprised at how your intensity and focus shoot up as your competitive spirit kicks in.

Three Down

Get three random shots up and in in a row to win your way off the green.

Five-Hole Coin Drill

Scatter five balls randomly around the green and play them into the same hole. Before playing each shot, walk onto the green and place a coin on your intended landing spot. Continue hitting from the same place until you can land a ball near the coin. (If it doesn't end up near the pin, move the coin and repeat until you've correctly determined the perfect landing spot for that shot.) Follow the same routine at all five locations. This drill will help you develop the ability to see your landing spot and predict rollout depending on the trajectory, shot choice, and lie.

Use the sample practice plan listed below to guide you as you create your plan in your journal.

SAMPLE 30-MINUTE FINESSE WEDGE TRAINING PLAN

Block Practice		
ACTIVITY	QUANTITY/TIME	GOALS
Mirror Drill	10 perfect repetitions	1. Check setup 2. Learn backswing plane 3. Learn face rotation
Stack Drill	5 perfect repetitions	Complete organized checklist of all setup fundamentals
Trail-Arm-Only Drill	5 perfect repetitions	Create awareness of sequence, release, and energy to the pin
Three-Trajectory Drill	2 sets of three shots	Develop an ability to hit three different trajectories to the same pin
Random Practice		
ACTIVITY	QUANTITY/TIME	GOALS
Scatter twenty-five balls, 1 to 30 yards from the green, Easter Egg-hunt style	15 minutes	Develop judgment regarding shot selection, lies, adaptations, running your process, and mental plan
Game Playing		
ACTIVITY	QUANTITY/TIME	GOALS
Play 21	10 minutes	Compete and perform with simulated pressure—and win your way off the green

CHAPTER 10

BUNKER SHOTS: TOUR TECHNIQUES FOR EVERY PLAYER

You **explode** *from sand, but quality bunker shots require many of the same* **finesse** *elements as short shots around the green.*

Tour pros make bunker play look easy, which is frustrating to weekend golfers, the majority of whom hemorrhage shots in the sand. During the normal course of play, some swings prove more valuable than others, and those from bunkers typically come with a hefty price tag: A properly struck sand shot can help you save par (or make birdie on a par-5 hole) while a bad one may lead to triple-bogey. As was the case with finesse wedges, you can learn to explode with the best of them if you're willing to train with discipline. In 2013, three of my Tour clients ranked in the top 10 in sand saves: Ben Crane (6th, 63.1%), Kevin Chappell (8th, 61.7%), and Cameron Tringale (10th, 61.5%).

Great bunker players calmly walk into the sand and execute with confidence. I know you can, too. The first step? A quick review of the three-step process for long-term, sustainable success:

1. Understand and believe in your method.
2. Know how to train to master your method and develop essential skills.
3. Feel and think like a champion so you can trust your method and skills.

You've already learned the principles of effective training and developing a strong mental game in previous chapters. These axioms apply to any area of the game that you're trying to improve, including bunkers. Therefore, the trick to elevating your sand game is to first make sure that you understand and believe in your method, and to then create block-practice drills to perfect its execution. We'll start with the following three fundamentals for finesse bunker shots—the unilateral keys to producing consistently solid contact from the sand.

FINESSE BUNKER-SWING FUNDAMENTAL NO. 1:

Expose the Loft and Bounce of the Club

The secret to great bunker play is to understand the correct way to "expose" the loft and bounce of the club through impact. Very few amateur players know how to do it, and they therefore suffer from an inability to create proper height and spin or muster any measure of consistency and control. Using loft and bounce correctly produces a noticeable *thump* at impact. It's the sound of the sole smacking the sand. (All you generally hear when you dig in with the leading edge are your own gasps and groans.) The most reliable way to expose the bounce and loft is to adjust your setup and swing for finesse.

Set up like a Bear

Addressing the ball correctly is a big part of mastering bunker play, and it involves several fundamental details. The goal of your setup is to create lower-body stability and add effective loft to the club. Follow these instructions while

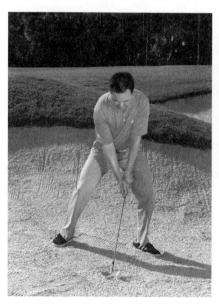

The finesse bunker-swing setup.   PGA Tour player Charlie Wi.

referencing the photos on the preceding page of PGA Tour player Charlie Wi, one of the best bunker players of his generation:

Grip: Hold the club using a finesse grip, with the V formed by the thumb and forefinger of your trail hand pointing at your sternum. Perform the putter-grip drill from page 46 to ensure that you're gripping the club with the fingers of your trail hand and that you're "on top" of the handle.

Stance: Make it wide—shoulder-width, at the very least—and turn both feet out about 45 degrees. Flex your knees so that it feels as though you're sitting, or "settling" your weight into the front of both thighs, and that you're balanced a little more over your front foot. Combining a wide, flared stance with the feel of sitting makes it difficult to rotate your hips. Excessive hip turn is an absolute killer in sand.

Club: As you widen and sit, lower your hands to just above knee height and allow the clubface to rotate open (clockwise for a right-handed golfer) as you do so. With this low-hands address, it'll feel like the shaft is lying much flatter than normal. Go with it. Obviously, you can't get this feeling if you're standing too close to the ball—you may have to back up a bit. It's OK—the only time you stand farther away from the ball than you do when hitting a sand shot is when you're hitting driver off the tee.

Alignment: When using a wedge with 56 to 60 degrees of loft (standard for most greenside bunker shots), keep your stance square to the target line or open it slightly. Traditional instruction suggests aligning your body significantly to the left of the target (to the right for left-handers). I think it's a mistake, since a wide-open stance in the sand prevents the proper delivery and release of the club.

Ball position: This, along with shaft lean (which is affected by ball position), needs to be worked through individually, because different positions aid different swing and contact patterns. Read this chapter so that you have a clear concept of what a fundamentally sound finesse-wedge setup and swing look like, then perform the following bunker-setup test to determine your optimal ball and handle position:

Bunker-Setup Test

Set up as described above without a ball. Execute a finesse bunker swing and splash sand onto the green. Check your sand divot and take note of where the club entered the sand relative to the position of your feet. Do this a few times, or until you have a good idea of where your typical entry point occurs. The best ball position for you, all other things being equal, is about two inches ahead of your natural entry point. Use your body as reference for this spot; for example, "middle of my stance" or "across from my lead heel."

If your natural entry point is significantly behind the center of your stance, your swing is too shallow. Try "flexing" more into your lead thigh and pointing your lead knee toward the target. Also, press the handle forward until you create about 10 degrees of shaft lean. Repeat the test and mark your new entry point.

If your natural entry point is far forward in your stance (closer to the heel of your front foot) and you're taking *a lot* of sand, your swing is too steep. Distribute your weight more evenly, point your trail knee away from the target (like you're riding a horse), and check that the shaft is straight up and down, or even leaning a degree back. Stick to this process and you'll nail the ideal finesse bunker setup for your particular swing.

Explode with a Finesse Sequence

The body turn and arm extension that help you add power in your full swing will hurt you in the sand. A great bunker swing features little or no lower-body movement and weight shift, along with a narrow arm swing. These combine to produce a steep backswing arc, which is ideal, because releasing the club past your body through impact (finesse sequencing) is a shallowing element. As was the case with the finesse wedge swing, balancing steep moves with shallow ones is key for optimal performance.

Keeping your lower body stable and letting the club pass your body is also what exposes the bounce (i.e., it positions the club in a way that allows the sole

Great bunker players like Charlie Wi balance steep-swing elements (narrow arc) with shallow ones (letting the clubhead release past the body) for optimal contact in sand.

to properly interact with the sand), and swinging this way also provides the added benefit of increased effective loft. Loft and speed create height and spin, the hallmark traits of pro-style bunker shots. In the sand, your lower body provides stability and balance. It isn't used for power generation like it is in a full swing, so you'll probably feel as though your upper body and arms are doing all the work.

FINESSE BUNKER-SWING FUNDAMENTAL NO. 2:

Enter and Exit for a "Thump"

As mentioned previously, old-school instruction suggests that you open your stance at address and swing along your toe line, cutting across the ball. This functions to some degree, but it isn't optimal, because you have to hold onto your release to make the ball fly toward the target. It also produces cut spin, so the ball won't bounce straight when it hits the green.

Important! The best bunker players in the world can actually draw the ball ever so slightly from sand, but not by swinging from inside-out or with a toe-over-heel release. It happens because the lie angle created by the low-hands position and the large amount of effective loft created by the proper release (clubhead passing the hands) produces a closed face relative to the path.

It's confusing, I know, especially since good wedge players splash sand from slightly outside-to-in relative to the target line. The easiest way to explain it is via a checkpoint, at a position in the swing instructors call "P6." P6 is the point in the swing when the shaft is parallel to the ground in the downswing and even with the hands. Note this position in frame two of the sequence of Charlie Wi below.

Charlie Wi creating max speed in a bunker in the right place—about a foot in front of the ball.

Delivering the club from this proper P6 position and then letting the club pass your stable lower body produces the perfect angle of attack and club alignments for performance. It's also what gives you the *thump* sound as the club enters the sand and a long, shallow divot. As for the exit, check frame 4. The clubface is open, which can only happen if you bend your lead wrist back so that it cups (extension) while simultaneously rotating your trail arm clockwise (supination). Soft and relaxed arms are key in this regard.

I'm aware that technical information such as this isn't worth much without a practical way to master it. This is where my "Seve Drill" comes in handy. It's well known that Seve Ballesteros grew up practicing on the beaches of Pedreña, Spain, with just a 3-iron to his name. Through his own volition, he intuitively found a way to create enough loft and bounce to hit solid shots from sand with that club, and he did it by using the setup and swing guidelines I've just discussed: He set up like a bear, lowered the handle at address, and used a finesse sequence to enter and exit the sand for a *thump*.

My goal as a teacher is to create simplicity and replace words with feels. Here's how I help students feel what Seve did: I hand you an 8-iron and ask you to hit a high, soft-spinning bunker shot to a short pin. How would you do it? If you're a player with an innate feel for the clubhead, you'll intuitively recognize the value of the finesse bunker fundamentals. This is essentially the Seve Drill. Lower the handle to create loft. Release the club past your body to create spin. Keep your lower body quiet to avoid hitting a shank. Swing in the right sequence to create finesse. View the sequence of pictures of me executing the Seve Drill below.

| 1. Wide stance and low hands to maximize loft. | 2. Arms-dominated backswing with very little lower-body movement. | 3. Clubhead back in front of the body with the clubface open. | 4. Clubhead passing the body through impact, creating maximum loft. | 5. Clubhead exiting under the lead shoulder. |

Seve Ballesteros could hit high-flying, high-spinning, ultra-soft bunker shots using a 3-iron. His secret? Finesse bunker fundamentals.

It's nature *and* nurture. Seve didn't rise to short-game stardom solely on the wings of his unique gifts. Circumstance also played a role. His environment taught him to manage the tools he was given to produce the shots he wanted to create. Tom Pernice Jr., Kevin Chappell, James Driscoll, and Charley Hoffman all use the Seve Drill as part of their weekly block-bunker practice. Perhaps you should, too.

Expert at Work!

Watch PGA Tour player James Driscoll execute the Seve Drill to perfection in a special video. Visit jsegolfacademy.com/index.php/james-driscoll.

FINESSE BUNKER-SWING FUNDAMENTAL NO. 3:

Feel the Speed in the Correct Place

One of the most common bunker-swing errors I see from amateurs is transitioning too quickly from backswing to downswing and then decelerating. This inhibits a proper release and creates a "chunk" mishit—the clubhead sticks in the sand while negating energy to the point where the ball remains in the bunker. The correct feeling is that you're slowly building up speed until the moment you let the club swing past your body. In a good bunker swing, the clubhead reaches top speed *after* impact—about a foot in front of the ball. Commitment to feeling top speed after impact will aid your ability to release and accelerate the club past your body, then rehinge it upward in your follow-through. You did it correctly if the clubhead is higher than your head at the finish.

Here's hoping that the fundamentals and drills described in this chapter have not only erased some of your misconceptions about bunker play, but that they've painted a clearer picture of the correct technique and, more important, that the technique is working for you as you practice it. It needs to work! There's no point in discussing distance control, adaptations for different conditions, and training plans until your contact patterns are consistent. Next up: fixes to your common bunker-swing flaws.

Expert at Work!

Watch PGA Tour player Charlie Wi execute one of the best bunker swings you'll ever see in a special video. Visit jsegolfacademy.com/index.php/charlie-wi.

Record the keys to a world-class bunker swing, including the components of your setup. Where's the ball? How much does the shaft lean forward at address? Define everything so that you can commit to your fundamentals and work toward mastery. In your own words, note the feels when you execute correctly. Check the example below.

FINESSE BUNKER SWING

TECHNICAL COMMITMENTS:

1. Set up to expose the loft and bounce of the club.
   Remember to turn your feet out and sit!
   It feels like I'm on a stool.
   Lower the handle and check your ball position each time!

2. Exit and enter for a thump.
   Keep my lower body underneath—use my legs for stability, not power.
   Make sure to keep the cup in the lead wrist for the entire motion.

3. Feel the speed in the right place.
   Accelerate smoothly past the ball.
   When the club exits under my armpit in the follow-through, I feel a slight stretch across my back.
   The clubhead should be above my head in the finish.

CHAPTER 11

GREENSIDE BUNKER FLAWS AND FIXES

Most faults in the bunker occur at the setup, creating a domino or cascading effect of errors. Mastery in the sand starts at address.

Working on the fundamentals described in the previous chapter will no doubt get you thumping the sand like a pro. You'll have to practice, and it will take discipline, but you'll get there. You may encounter some bumps in the road, what I like to call the "fatal flaws" of bunker play. It all starts with your setup. Get this right first before working on the following swing mistakes.

The Fatal Flaws

FLAW NO. 1: Bad setup.

How you know you have it: Inconsistent contact—you rarely hear the *thump* at impact.

Why you have it: Your angle of attack is too steep or too shallow, depending on your setup error(s).

Effect on contact: Inconsistency—your contact is all over the map.

How to fix it: Use Setup Checks.

Reread my setup guidelines from the last chapter. At home, rehearse your address position in front of a mirror, focusing on one fundamental at a time. Note the setups that don't come naturally to you. Those are the ones you need to work on. Check your setup in a mirror regularly to make sure you're really executing. Remember, there's a difference between feel and real.

When you're at your practice facility, create "Setup Checks," which are visible lines in the sand that guide you out of your setup errors and into a solid address position. Follow these steps:

Step 1: Using your club, draw a line along your target line. Place a ball just inside it. Call this line No. 1.

Step 2: Draw a parallel line close to where your toes will be at address. This is line No. 2.

Step 3: Draw a third line (perpendicular to lines 1 and 2) from the ball through your stance.

Step 4: Draw a fourth line running from just inside the ball to the big toe of your lead foot.

Take your stance. Check that the ball position matches what you determined in your entry-point test in the previous chapter. (For example, if your best ball position is off your lead heel, make sure line No. 3 points at your lead heel.) Use line No. 2 to align your feet, pointing your stance straight down the line or slightly open. Hover the club above the sand and behind the ball. Check that the leading edge matches line No. 4, which will correctly set the club in a slightly open position. Now swing, making sure to splash the sand. The resulting divot or sand displacement tells you a lot about your faults.

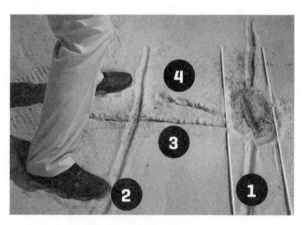

SETUP CHECKS

Line 1 = Target line
Line 2 = Stance line
Line 3 = Ball position
Line 4 = Clubface angle
Sticks = Ideal swing
path

The divot shouldn't point directly down line No. 1 (target line), but rather 10 degrees from out-to-in (as shown by the alignment sticks in the photo). If it does point down the line, you're delivering the club too far from the inside. Go back to the Seve Drill (page 119) and learn the correct sequencing and clubhead/handle relationship in the delivery from the master. Use these Setup Checks regularly as part of your block practice.

FLAW NO. 2: Clubhead digging too deeply into the sand.

How you know you have it: You leave shots in the bunker.

Why you have it: Your angle of attack is too steep.

Effect on contact: Fat shots that don't go far enough.

How to fix it: Try my Bunker Trail-Arm-Only Drill.

STEP 1: Get into your bunker setup and address the ball. Remove your lead hand from the grip and place it on your lead thigh. Use the feeling of your hand on your thigh to remind you to maintain pressure on your lead leg all the way into the finish.

STEP 2: Swing the club back using only your trail arm.

STEP 3: Swing down and "throw" the clubhead under the ball. Using your trail arm makes it easier to release the clubhead past your body so that you don't drag the handle into impact, a move that causes the clubhead to dig deep in the sand.

STEP 4: Internalize both the sequence at the start of the downswing and the release of the clubhead as it passes your body. Rehinge the club in your follow-through so that the clubhead is above your head at the finish. Repeat five times, then try it with both hands on the handle and replicate the same feel.

FLAW NO. 3: Entering the sand too far behind the ball.

How you know you have it: The ball stays in the bunker.

Why you have it: Your angle of attack is too steep or too shallow, depending on your error(s).

Effect on contact: Fat shots.

How to fix it: Move energy toward the target so you can release the clubhead.

If you're leaving the ball in the bunker, your entry point is likely too far behind the ball. This may be the result of any one of a number of errors. You could be hitting too far behind the ball because of excess coil and width in your backswing, but the more likely culprit is that you're reversing your weight shift on the downswing. Remember, energy always moves toward the target in the short game.

To fix this problem, repeat the Stork Drill from page 60 in the sand. Make five swings without a ball while maintaining pressure in your lead leg throughout your backswing, and increase this pressure all the way to the finish.

You also could be hanging onto your release (digging), which will make your delivery too steep and sharpen the leading edge of the club, limiting your use of bounce. As a fix, perform the bunker Trail-Arm-Only Drill (page 125).

Lastly, you may be generating speed in the wrong place, which, as described in the previous chapter, forces you to stall out your arm swing and upper-body rotation. To fix this error, follow these steps:

1. Make a mark in the sand a foot in front of the ball.
2. Turn your club upside down and grip it around the hosel.
3. Make five swings above the ball. Start smoothly in your downswing accelerating the club so that you create a *whoosh* sound out where the mark in the sand is. You should feel that the maximum speed of the club is in front of the ball.
4. Commit to this feeling and be sure to rehinge the club above your head in the finish.

FLAW NO. 4: Skulling.
How you know you have it: The ball flies too low and won't stay on the green.
Why you have it: Your angle of attack is too shallow.
Effect on contact: Thin shots.
How to fix it: Perfect your angle of attack.

This debilitating shot is often caused by failing to shift laterally while also casting the club too early in the downswing. This is a common full-swing motor pattern among amateurs. You know you have it if you like "sweeping" the ball off the tee with your driver but hate "pinching" it against the ground with an iron. To get out of this pattern and remove the shallowing elements, try my Stick-It Drill.

Step 1: Draw a straight line in the sand from six inches in front of the ball back to your stance.
Step 2: Swing to the top of your backswing and pause for a few seconds.

Step 3: Swing down in slow motion, shifting your weight and maintaining the angle in your wrists through the first foot of your downswing. Pause again. If you did it correctly, the butt of the club will point at the line in the sand and your swing will be much steeper.

Step 4: Swing the club past your stable lower body. This drill teaches you to simply "stick it in and let it pass." *Au revoir,* skulls! Repeat the drill five times, then remove the pauses and try to swing with the same feels.

Charlie Wi "sticking" it before allowing the clubhead to pass his body.

FLAW NO. 5: Inconsistent entry.
How you know you have it: You follow a chunked bunker shot with a skull.
Why you have it: You haven't developed the skill to "throw" the club into the sand at the right place.
Effect on contact: Thin shots and fat shots.
How to fix it: Try my Two-Shot-Penalty Drill.

All great bunker players have developed the essential skill of consistently entering the sand in the correct place, which is approximately an inch and a half behind the ball. Anyone can improve this skill regardless of their ability by adding the Two-Shot-Penalty drill to their block practice. (Tom Pernice Jr. calls it the "Seve Drill" because he saw Ballesteros do it often during his training. Since I have my own Seve Drill [page 119], I changed the name. Sorry, Tom.)

Set up to your ball in the bunker as you normally would, but instead of hovering the club in the air, go ahead and push the heel down in the sand where you want the club to enter. Doing this during play comes with a two-shot penalty—hence the name of the drill—but it's perfectly OK for practice. As you swing back, focus intently on the mark made by the club at address and do your best to hit it as you enter the sand. This drill not only trains you to externally focus on the correct entry point, it gives you a sense of how the club should hinge up in the backswing and unhinge in the delivery. Hit fifteen shots this way and make it a regular part of your block training.

FLAW NO. 6: Shanking.
How you know you have it: You shouldn't have to ask.
Why you have it: Your path is off or your downswing is out of sequence.
Effect on contact: You can't find the middle of the clubface.

There are two ways to shank the ball out of the bunker. The first is a result of errors in your sequence. If you spin your hips in the downswing before you get the club back down in front of your body, the handle of the club will "drag" as it moves into impact. Since you opened the clubface at address, adding spin and drag means very little if it will be facing the ball at impact, leaving you only the hosel as a contact point.
How to fix it: Try my Barstool Drill.

Find a standard-height swiveling barstool. Sit on the front edge of the stool and execute mock bunker swings. Doing this instills the proper feeling of the arms moving before your hips (finesse sequence) and your lower body providing stability so that the clubhead can release back in front of your body with the clubface looking at the ball.

The more common cause of a shank is swinging above or below the proper plane. You can solve either path error with an easy block-practice drill.
How to fix it: Try my Railroad Track Drill.

Place a ball in the sand and set an alignment stick on both sides of it about seven inches apart, railroad-track style. Point the rails (sticks) 10 degrees left of your target line (the ideal path). Remove the ball and make slow-motion swings until you develop an awareness of the clubhead traveling through the channel formed by the track as you splash the sand. Go as slowly as needed to deliver the clubhead correctly. Making contact with either stick should tell you what the problem is. If you're striking the inside rail before you hit the sand, your swing is in-to-out and under the ideal plane. If you're striking the outside rail before you hit the sand, your swing is out-to-in and above plane. Swinging on plane is a skill you must develop to perform well. There's no wiggle room here. Once you complete five successful swings in slow motion, replace the sticks with lines drawn in the sand to remove the risk of injury, and swing at a normal pace. After you make five successful swings through the lines, introduce a ball and repeat.

STEP 1: Set up your track.

STEP 2: Swing through the channel created by the track and splash the sand without striking the rails.

JOURNAL WORK

In the bunker section of your journal, record the three bunker-swing fundamentals and the drills associated with fixing any problems that you're having trying to execute them. Using your own language, record the feelings you get when performing each drill correctly, like an artist describing a masterpiece that he or she has created. Being able to crawl outside your body and both see and feel yourself execute a great shot will go a long way toward owning your technique and mastering what you do.

CHAPTER 12

SPECIALTY BUNKER SHOTS AND BUNKER SWING TRAINING PLAN

Don't be satisfied with just getting it out, get it close from every circumstance. A master bunker player is an artist who can paint with any size brush.

A bunker is called a hazard for a reason, and your strategy should prioritize avoiding them at all costs. And don't be fooled by what you see on TV, which prefers to show the good bunker shots rather than the bad ones. Even pros find them challenging. Consider the following averages:

LIE	SCRAMBLING %	STROKE EFFICIENCY
In the bunker	59.3	2.41
Around the green	85.0	2.16

These numbers, from the 2013 PGA Tour season on shots of 10 yards and less, show that on average, hitting into greenside sand comes with roughly a quarter-stroke penalty. The message? Be smart when it comes to evaluating yourself and avoiding situations that stress your game. Easier said than done, I know, because bunkers are *everywhere*, and obviously you're going to find them from time to time in your golf career. The trick to is to avoid them when you can and master them when you can't.

In this chapter you'll learn how to prepare and execute from different sand conditions and lies. Although there's no substitute for experience, implementing the tricks and specialty shots described below will both speed up the learning curve and help you put your competition to shame.

THE ART OF CONTROLLING DISTANCE

There are multiple ways to control how far you hit a specific bunker shot. Some of them are dangerous and difficult, while others are quite easy. I'm all for easy! I'm not a fan of squaring the clubface, shallowing the angle of attack or striking the sand a little closer to the ball to help it fly farther. These traditional techniques work in theory, but each invites an increased probability of a disastrous miss. There's no need. The goal is to produce great shots or acceptable misses. My suggestion? Develop a repeatable sand setup and swing (Chapter 10) and simply change the club or the speed of your motion to vary the shot distance.

As a starting point, create base carry yardages for each of your sand clubs. Jump into the practice bunker at your home course or regular practice facility and start making comfortable, rhythmic swings with your most-lofted wedge. Keep at it until you hit five quality bunker shots. Compute an average distance for these, disregarding extreme outliers, and then repeat the process for each club all the way up to your 9-iron. Record the yardages in your journal. Mine go like this:

> Lob wedge: 12 yards
> Sand wedge: 18 yards
> Gap wedge: 25 yards
> Pitching wedge: 32 yards
> 9-iron: 38 yards

The beauty in changing clubs to change distance from a bunker is that you only have to master one basic motion. To generate yardages between your base numbers, simply add or reduce arm speed. This is where feel comes in. Pull the correct club, consider your base number relative to the landing spot, then engage with the target and feel the speed that matches your picture. This is the process used by Tom Pernice Jr., Ben Crane, and all of the great bunker players I've coached. A side benefit to this technique is that it allows you to swing using a manageable rhythm; there's no need to really go hard at the ball. Players who overswing tend to use too much lower-body action, which, as you learned in the last chapter, is the quick way to hit a bad bunker shot. Using your lower body as a power source changes the position of the bottom of your swing arc and the way the club interacts with the sand in a detrimental way.

When you have to hit a shot shorter than your shortest stock reference yardage (say, 10 yards or less), choke down to the bottom of the grip, lower the handle a little more than normal, and shorten your backswing a bit. Shortening the club by choking down allows you to hit smaller shots while maintaining an aggressive mindset and keeping the speed of your swing in the correct place.

A Note on Height

Players often ask me how to hit higher sand shots so that they can carry the lip on a steep-faced bunker. True, a tall lip creates a shot-management issue and priority number one is to get the ball out, but even an 8-iron produces enough height to carry the ball out of 90 percent of the bunkers you'll see. (This is true only if you set up and deliver the club properly and expose the loft and bounce.) I can still picture Seve popping up soft 3-irons out of a practice bunker higher than most of us could carry with a sand wedge. With my techniques and a little practice, you'll get that good, too (although you should probably stick to 8-iron on down).

Interestingly, because of its head shape and lie angle, a less-lofted club such as an 8-iron produces "cut" spin when using the finesse setup and swing, which means that a right-handed player needs to move their landing spot and body alignment more to the left, or open, to allow for it.

THE ART OF ADAPTING

Even during the course of a single round, you'll experience odd bunker lies and shot conditions. Knowing how to adapt to them will keep your numbers from ballooning. Here are the solutions to common lie situations sand conditions. Familiarize yourself with the general techniques for handling them, then integrate them into your random-practice training sessions for the full effect.

Hard Versus Soft Sand

Soft or thick sand makes the ball come out slow, while firm, compacted sand adds distance or makes the ball come out fast. For this reason, you need to slightly adjust your base carry numbers and feel for distance (similar to how you adjust your full-swing numbers when you play on a really hot day or at altitude). In addition, consider the bounce. There's one bounce option that's best for the situation and that will help you select the right club. In Chapter 3, I gave you recommendations for the ideal wedge-set makeup. To reiterate, having a sand wedge with a lot of bounce (11 to 14 degrees) and a lob wedge with less (4 to 7 degrees) provides the perfect combination of weapons to combat both soft and firm sand. In soft, loose sand, you need more bounce, so you should go with your sand wedge, not your lob wedge. Its greater bounce angle and reduced loft gives you a twofer. More bounce reduces the amount of dig; less loft helps make up for the fact that loose sand absorbs energy from the delivery and causes the ball to fly short. As a rule, defer in soft sand to a less-lofted club, and keep the face open at address.

The same twofer exists when the sand is firm and compact, a situation that calls for less bounce and more loft. Your 60-degree wedge is the perfect choice. Remember to adjust your base yardages accordingly. This means that in order to hit a club to its stock number, you'll either need a little less speed or a shortened club. Don't square the club's face in this situation. It'll only cause the ball to go farther and make it difficult to stop on the green. Your one job in the bunker is to deliver the club completely under the ball, and in extremely firm, baked-out conditions, I'd suggest steepening the angle of attack by choking down on the club and shifting your weight and handle position more toward your lead thigh at address, as I discussed in Chapter 5. This will help the club hinge up more abruptly in your backswing and allow you to deliver the club under the ball.

Downhill Lies

This is a difficult shot for everybody, including professionals. The adaptation you make for a downhill lie in the sand is the same as for a downhill lie in the grass, and also similar to the technique just mentioned for extreme, hard-packed sand conditions. Widen your stance, point the toe of your lead foot down the hill, and let the hill push your head, handle, and weight into your lead thigh. This delofts the club, so make sure you choose your lob wedge or most lofted club, regardless of the distance. Play the ball forward, open the clubface, and lower the handle so you have enough effective loft on the club to carry the ball over the lip of the bunker. Your backswing will feel more abrupt than normal due to these setup changes. Maintain lower-body stability in your lead thigh throughout the downswing and deliver the club with a slight fade mentality.

How to Handle a Downhill Lie

Create angle at address, maximize clubhead loft, and keep pressure in your lead thigh.

Uphill Lies

Although I recommend shallowing out your path on an uphill lie in grass, I don't recommend it for the same lie in a bunker, because if we overdo it even just a little bit, you'll suffer a debilitating miss that'll cost you several shots. Severe bunker upslopes cause the ball to fly higher and shorter, so adjust your stock carry number accordingly and drop down a club.

Narrow and open your stance more than usual as you set up to the ball. Keep your balance even and your spine straight up and down—it shouldn't lean back or forward. You're set up correctly if your lead leg is flexed more than your trail leg. Open the clubface a little less than you would for your stock bunker shot, and visualize the heel and handle exiting more to the left or across the slope (more to the left for a right-handed golfer). The club will dig a little more than normal, but if you enter the sand an inch and a half behind the ball as you usually do, the ball will pop out predictably with a high trajectory and a soft landing.

I call this the "Curtis Strange Shot," named after the two-time U.S. Open champion. Curtis taught it to Tom Pernice Jr., and then Tom taught it to me. Now I'm teaching it to you. I guess consistently borrowing from the greats is just my thing!

How to Handle an Uphill Lie

Despite the slope, feel balanced and centered and picture the heel exiting left (for right-handers).

Sidehill Lies

Adaptations for sidehill lies in the sand are identical to those you make on sidehill lies in the grass. For a ball below your feet, widen out and get as close to the ball as possible so that the heel of the club doesn't catch the turf first. Set up and swing with a fade mentality, and remember that fades go short, so add a little energy to your swing. For a ball above your feet, open the face more to counteract the lie angle (and properly aim the face), add energy to your swing, and swing with a draw mentality.

Buried Lies

When the ball is buried in the sand, your goals change. Instead of playing offense, your objective is to get the ball somewhere on the green and give yourself a putt. That being said, you still want some measure of control when it comes

The chunk-and-run shot from a buried lie.

to spin and distance. I teach two different shots to escape buried lies based on what you want the ball to do once it hits the green. Both are bonafide shot-savers.

If you have a longer shot with a lot of green to work with, and you want the ball to tumble forward and run, you can play the "Chunk-and-Run." Use either your sand or gap wedge, depending on the amount of energy you want to impart to the shot. Stand taller and closer to the ball with a square, shoulder-width stance. Position the ball opposite your back foot. Keep the face square and your hands in the middle of your stance, which will create 10 degrees or more of shaft lean. This will steepen the angle of attack and sharpen the leading edge of the club, helping it to dig completely under the ball and dislodge it from the sand. Make a big enough backswing so that your wrists hinge completely. Maintain lower-body stability and release the clubhead down into the sand two inches behind the ball with smooth acceleration. The fact that the club digs into the sand will limit your follow-through—make sure that the sand is what decelerates the club, not anything you do. If you enter the sand in the correct place, the ball should pop out with medium height and have no backspin, which will allow it to roll across the green.

The more difficult buried-lie shot is when you need it to pop up softly and stop it more quickly when it hits the green. To pull this difficult shot off, play the "Two-Sided Axe," which will provide maximum loft and an extremely steep angle of attack. Start by aligning your feet and body 20 degrees closed to the target line. Maintain the wide stance, open face, and low handle of a normal shot. Swing as much as 30 degrees out-to-in relative to your stance line. Pick the

The Two-Sided Axe from a buried lie.

club straight up and out in your backswing. Let your elbows fold, as though you're swinging an axe, and then unfold them to deliver the club aggressively across your body and back down into the sand. Obviously, there'll be little to no follow-through. Performed correctly, the ball will pop out higher than normal and with a little "check" backspin, which will prevent the ball from running too far once it lands.

It's great to know what to do on really difficult shots such as these, but I'd prefer that you focus your energy and time on mastering the simple and more common ones.

Greenside Bunker Training Plan

A world-class bunker training plan follows the same structure laid out for your finesse wedges in Chapter 7. Again, perform your block practice first to confirm your execution of the fundamentals, then cultivate your skills by practicing in a random manner using your full process and championship-feeling strategies. A twenty- to thirty-minute training session is sufficient. Part of your block practice is dictated by an awareness of the flaws and the drills designed to fix them. Don't forget to finish with a game or two at the end. I've listed some of my favorites here.

Charlie Wi and I working on adapting to different lie conditions prior to the 2013 Honda Classic.

INTENTFUL PRACTICE BUNKER GAMES

Play Seven

From the same location in the bunker, play one ball to three different holes. Complete each hole by holing out with your putter. To win the game, you must complete all three in seven strokes or less (or eight strokes for higher-handicap players). Keep track of your scores in your journal and always strive for a personal best.

Six-Up

Challenge a player of similar skill level to a bunker-shot shootout. Same rules and scoring as in your finesse wedge practice, but this time randomly toss the balls into a spot in the bunker instead of around the green.

Throw Darts

Play nine random short-game holes (three easy, three medium, and three difficult) from a greenside bunker with one ball. Use the same scoring as in your finesse wedge practice. Tournament-level players can achieve a minimum bunker Dart score of thirteen points. Yours may differ based on your skill level. As always, use your score to set goals, track progress, and gun for a personal best.

Elimination

Choose any hole. From the bunker, play shots from the following six lies: 1) downslope, 2) upslope, 3) ball above your feet, 4) ball below your feet, 5) buried, and 6) normal. Play from the same position until you hit a shot that finishes within three steps of the cup. Once you've done that, that area is eliminated. Move on to the next lie condition and repeat the process, and keep at it until you eliminate all six areas. Your score is the total number of balls it takes you to finish the game.

Bunker-Practice Accountability

Beyond writing your technical keys and training plan in your journal, record your score or performance in the games you play, as well as anything you've learned during your practice session. It's a great day when you can learn something in practice that'll help you perform better for the rest of your playing career. Remember that bad shots are opportunities to learn and grow. Fight to master your fundamentals and improve your skills every day.

PGA Tour Confidential: Cameron Tringale

"At the beginning of every bunker session, whether it's on the practice green at home or on Sunday morning before the final round of a big tournament, I work on the same fundamentals. The first thing I always do in the bunker is to draw my setup-check lines in the sand. I hit into open space and just focus on every element of my address position. Since I have a way to set up the same way every time, my swing is the only variable.

"Next, I hit a handful of shots, working on rhythm and trying to find that elusive 'thump' sound. Once I get that sound and good contact four or five times in a row, I move away from my lines and just play a variety of shots to different pin locations. Getting the correct contact in bunkers is key—the rest is knowing which wedge to use, judging lies, etc. I like to experiment by trying to hit the same shot using different clubs. I also like to work on a variety of specialty shots: low, high, chunk-and-run, two-sided axe, downhill, uphill, etc. Before I leave the bunker, I challenge myself to get up and down three times in a row. This gives me the confidence that I can go out on the course and be prepared for any bunker shot that may come my way."

Use the sample practice plan below to help you formulate your own training regimen, and write it down in the bunker section of your journal. Remember to leave space to record your game scores and any artistic things you might have learned about your bunker game.

SAMPLE 25-MINUTE GREENSIDE BUNKER TRAINING PLAN

Block Practice		
ACTIVITY	QUANTITY/TIME	GOALS
Setup Checks	5 perfect repetitions	Confirmation of all setup fundamentals.
Seve Drill	5 perfect repetitions	Ensure proper finesse sequence. Get the feel of the hand/clubhead relationship of the release to maximize loft and spin.
Two-Shot-Penalty Drill	5 perfect repetitions	Develop awareness of entry point and the skill required to do it consistently.
Random Practice		
ACTIVITY	QUANTITY/TIME	GOALS
At least four clubs, random lies and distances, full process. Play every club and lie condition at least once.	10 minutes	Develop judgment regarding shot selection, lies, adaptations, running of process, and mental plan. Work on touch and feel for distance.
Game Playing		
ACTIVITY	QUANTITY/TIME	GOALS
Elimination	10 minutes	Compete and perform with simulated pressure—and win your way out of the bunker.

CHAPTER 13

DISTANCE WEDGES—TOUR TECHNIQUES FOR ANY PLAYER

If you're going to take advantage of the par 5s and short par 4s, and be able to play smart when you get in trouble and still score, it's critical to be a great distance wedge player.

A distance wedge is essentially a mini full swing using a power sequence. Recall that we eliminated the use of the archaic terms "chip" and "pitch" way back in Chapter 4 and replaced them with "finesse wedge" and "distance wedge." It makes sense to define short-game shots by their kinematic sequence, because the sequence, to a large degree, is responsible for producing the optimal contact, ball flight, spin rate, and power output required for all wedge shots.

A distance wedge shot normally carries in the range of 35 to 120 yards. The actual range will vary from player to player based on strength and skill, but this is a pretty good average. The top end of your distance wedge range should equal the carry distance of your pitching wedge on a full swing. Near the bottom end of the range, both finesse- and distance-wedge techniques are available to you. Base your decision as to which swing to use on shots from 30 to 50 yards on what produces the appropriate ball flight and spin rate for the shot you're facing.

For example, a 40-yard finesse wedge shot, hit with the right technique, launches relatively higher and with less spin than the same 40-yard shot hit using the distance wedge technique. On the finesse wedge shot, the ball hits the green and reacts and rolls more like a putt, while a distance wedge shot of the same distance produces that sexy sizzle of the ball checking on the green that you so often see on TV. In any case, as a short-game master, it's great to have choices that allow you to be in total control of your ball.

THE VALUE OF DISTANCE WEDGES TO SCORING

Distance wedge shots represent a huge opportunity when it comes to scoring. When you consider the percentage of putts you make from each distance on the green, there are plateau levels of performance when it comes to scoring. If you currently average a 30-foot putt following a distance wedge shot, and through hard work improve this average to 25 feet, it's likely that your scores won't change, even though you've improved your distance wedge accuracy by almost 17 percent! Why? Because there's very little difference in your putting average from those two distances. Of course, you don't hit all of your distance wedge shots your average distance all the time. You hit good ones and bad ones, the aggregate of which give you your average. Although the stat "Average Proximity" is the current matrix used to rank players' distance wedge skill on the PGA Tour, it doesn't begin to measure how these shots truly affect score. A better measure of skill would be the percentage of time a player can pull off a wedge shot that's so *fantastic* that it gains him or her a stroke compared to the competition, as well as the percentage of time he or she hits a shot that's so *horrible* that it causes him or her to lose a stroke to the competition (i.e., missing the green). It won't be long before there's a Strokes Gained statistic for distance wedges, which will be really helpful for me as I work with my Tour players.

The goal, as it has been throughout this book, is to make consistently solid contact in order to eliminate bad misses, as well as to develop the skills needed to control distance so that there's a high probability that you'll convert the putt. During practice, I try to quantify these plateau levels for my clients by having them think of a shot that ends up within two steps of their number as a birdie, within three to ten steps as a par, and within ten or more steps as a bogey. These are high standards, but they accurately reflect scoring reality. As such, it's important that you embrace that challenge.

Having a Plan

One of the things that Dave Pelz taught me when I worked for him was that almost every player can hit the ball reasonably straight when they have a lofted wedge in their hand, but the determining factor for success is being able to control distance. The main error in the short game is hitting the ball too far or too short; in the power game it's too far to the left or right. For this reason, distance control in your short game is the key variable. A properly struck 60-yard shot that flies 70 yards into a back bunker is still an awful result, regardless of how much you enjoyed it and how good it looked while it was in the air.

To be great, you must have a simple system that allows you to pick the correct shot, and to control both spin and trajectory so that you can consistently hit the ball the correct distance. If you don't like the thought of having a "system" because you're a "feel" player, to me that's just code for, "I don't have a clue what to do, and being a great distance wedge player is going to take too much focus and effort, so I'll hide behind the 'feel player' moniker." Of course you play by feel—we all do! The trick is to own a plan that complements your feel and that helps you develop touch so you can execute at the highest level. Not only does my system work, it's Tour-proven: Nick Watney, Tom Pernice Jr., and Kevin Chappell have all been at the top of one of the three distance wedge stat categories on the PGA Tour in recent years. They've mastered the system, and so can you.

Distance Wedge Matrix

In Chapter 3, I recommended a wedge-set makeup of two, three, or four wedges based on the carry number of your full pitching wedge, with yardage gaps of no more than 20 yards. Let's say you carry four wedges: pitching wedge, gap wedge, sand wedge, and lob wedge. You already have four known full-swing numbers. It's important to note that these numbers represent carry yardages on properly struck shots, not the total distance the ball travels. You need to be very precise to get the ball up and in, and thinking in terms of total distance doesn't cut it.

In addition to your four known full-swing numbers, you should create two more for each wedge, giving you a total of twelve. (If you carry three wedges, you'll have nine.) Get them by shortening your backswings with a slightly more rhythmic pace to impart less energy to the ball. How short? Using the image of a clock, I've always picked nine o'clock and 7:30 to represent the lead-arm position at the top of the backswing. I.K. Kim calls her backswing benchmarks "three-quarters" and "one-half." I have students who prefer to use their armpit and belly button as guides. I really don't care what you call them or what you use as long as you can repeat them consistently. Your distance wedge backswing benchmarks must feel so comfortable that you can hit them in your sleep. After doing this, your numbers might look something like this:

CLUB SELECTION				HIGHER TRAJECTORY HIGHER SPIN
PITCHING WEDGE	GAP WEDGE	SAND WEDGE	LOB WEDGE	
130 YARDS	**115** YARDS	**98** YARDS	**80** YARDS	
112 YARDS	**90** YARDS	**70** YARDS	**58** YARDS	
80 YARDS	**65** YARDS	**52** YARDS	**38** YARDS	

SHOT SELECTION — FULL SWING / 9:00 SWING / 7:30 SWING

LOWER TRAJECTORY
LOWER SPIN

Sample Distance Wedge Matrix

How Distance Wedge Swings Differ from Full Swings

To produce your known numbers on demand, it's not enough to just shorten your backswing. You need to be locked in and consistent with both your downswing effort level and your finish position. Effort level is subjective, so you need to quantify it. When I coach, I always have my players make a normal-paced full swing (i.e., carry their pitching wedge its full distance), then say to them, "That represents a 9-out-of-10 effort for you. You could hit it a few yards farther if you had to (that would be a 10 out of 10), but don't, because you'll sacrifice control and consistency." I'll then instruct them to make a nine o'clock backswing and finish at their lead shoulder with a 7-out-of-10 effort. It might take a few repetitions focusing on downswing energy before they can lock onto the smooth, positive effort level I'm looking for. Being consistent with the effort is critical to my system. Without it, backswing length won't have the desired relevance to the distance you want the ball to travel and your touch will be inconsistent. Make evaluating your effort level part of your post-shot routine.

Other than effort level and the use of benchmarks, your distance wedge swing shouldn't be that different than your full swing, with three notable exceptions:

1. **A narrower stance.** Set up with your feet square to the target line and no more than 12 inches apart, with the ball in the middle of your stance.
2. **More weight over your front leg at address.** 55 percent will do. This is especially critical for players with a higher ball flight and those who struggle with fat and thin contact.
3. **A shift-free backswing.** As you swing to the top, maintain the weight distribution that you established at address. In a full swing, it's quite common for players to load into their trail leg on the backswing by letting their shoulder rotation push their upper body and head behind the ball, but you won't see them do this from 70 yards. There's simply not enough time to turn behind the ball on a little swing and then shift to get your center back on top of it by impact. If you do turn and load behind the ball, not only will your trajectory be too high, you'll also struggle with fat and thin misses.

Understanding Distance Wedge Ball Flight and Swing "Verticals"

To maximize control and consistency in varying conditions, the best distance wedge players typically "flight" the ball down a bit while creating enough spin to stop it quickly on the green despite the lower trajectory. This is done by using the correct kinematic sequence to produce power, properly delivering the club into the ball, and creating sufficient clubhead speed and friction between the clubface and the ball. You need sharp grooves and a clean lie to create maximum spin, which is why professional players change wedges each year. (Take note and consider doing likewise when the groove edges start to become noticeably worn.)

It's intuitive that more loft and more speed creates more spin, but how do you flight a lofted wedge? Remember that as the goals pertaining to the use of the club change, so does the technique. If you used your finesse sequence on a shot from 75 yards, not only would it be next to impossible to hit a lofted club that far, that movement would produce an extremely high ball flight that would be at the mercy of the vagaries of the wind. A stronger, more penetrating flight is more effective. To accomplish this, slightly deloft the club at impact by having the handle lead the clubhead through the ball. A power sequence and the proper blend of both lateral and rotary motion from your body in the downswing are necessary to deliver the club this way. The lateral shift not only moves the low point of your swing arc forward, but buys time for you to swing the handle back down in front of your body, which is key to getting the shaft to lean slightly forward at impact.

This is essentially the first phase of the downswing. The second phase is the rotary motion of the body through impact and the continuation of the arm swing. This motion creates what I call "verticals" in your swing. Think about the

Ben Crane Executing a Textbook Nine O'Clock Distance Wedge Swing.

SETUP: Ball positioned in the middle, weight slightly favoring lead leg.

BACKSWING: Hitting the nine o'clock benchmark, head position hasn't moved at all.

PHASE 1 OF DOWNSWING: Three to four inches of lateral shift as arms swing down in front of the body.

PHASE 2 OF DOWNSWING:
Rotary body motion (employing his verticals so he can strike the ball with his hands ahead).

MID-FOLLOW-THROUGH:
Energy flowing to the pin while covering the ball with his trail side.

WORLD-CLASS FINISH:
Smooth, positive acceleration up to the finish line.

club's interaction with the turf for a minute: Your hands are ahead at impact and your weight is moving into your lead leg. It seems like this arrangement has created the potential for you to "dig a trench" with your wedge, and although taking a small divot is fine, this isn't what you see on TV. Why? When your body rotates in the second phase of the downswing, two things happen: 1) your lead leg begins to straighten (upward movement) as the hip turns back over the lead heel; and 2) the handle of the club ever so slightly follows suit as the lead shoulder rotates up and back around your head. Both of these verticals shallow your angle attack, allowing you to have your hands ahead of the clubhead at impact and your swing center forward without being too steep and digging a trench. Essentially, you've paired two steepening elements (stacked backswing and lateral downswing shift) with the two shallowing elements embedded in the verticals. The net effect is perfect contact and a controlled ball flight.

Expert at Work!

Watch PGA Tour Player Ben Crane explain how he hits a perfect nine o'clock distance wedge in a special video. Visit jsegolfacademy.com/index.php/ben-crane.

Create Your Known Numbers

With the preceding guidance on technique, you're ready to establish your known numbers. You're going to need feedback on how far each ball travels, so you'll need decent balls that are similar to those you typically play. Follow these steps:

Step 1: Go to the end of the range (or even a field in your neighborhood) and walk out targets every 10 yards, starting at 30 yards out up to your full pitching-wedge carry number. (The players I coach on Tour all travel with lightweight, stackable agility cones for this purpose.) I'm aware that this will require some planning and effort, but good players are willing to do anything and everything that's necessary to improve. Make it happen.

Step 2: After you warm up through a full 7-iron, make five great swings to your nine o'clock benchmark, giving each one 7-out-of-10 effort through the ball and consistently finishing up to your lead shoulder. Throw out the outliers and note your average carry numbers.

Step 3: Repeat the process for all of your wedges and write the carry yardages down on the back of the shaft with a Sharpie. Place a piece of Scotch Tape over the numbers so they don't wear off. Also note them in your journal in the distance wedge section. Eventually, it should look something like the sample Distance Wedge Matrix shown earlier in this chapter.

Step 4: Repeat steps 2 and 3 using your 7:30 benchmark.

These numbers and swing distances are only reference points. They're not and shouldn't be your only swing choices. Almost every shot you face will ultimately "feel" a little more or a little less than a stock benchmark shot, which will give you tens if not a hundred swings. Regardless of which swing you use, finish in the same place every time. End your swing with your hands near the logo on your lead chest with a 7-out-of-10 effort. Keeping your finish consistent

Your distance wedge finish position is a constant. End every swing with your hands near the logo on your shirt.

allows you to add or subtract distance from any known number by simply adjusting your backswing length.

As with all shots where the ball is compressed, ground and atmospheric conditions affect the distance a ball will fly. Your base yardages are based on normal conditions, but if it gets extremely hot or you find yourself at elevation, you'll need to note how far your base shots fly that week in practice and adjust accordingly. The pros I coach check their numbers on the Tuesday of a tournament week as they travel from one environment to another. Knowing exactly how much the conditions affect their distances gives them a competitive advantage over those that don't put in the work and just guess.

Choosing the Correct Shot

The centerpiece of my plan is to control both the trajectory and spin so that your ball will "one hop and stop" when it lands on the green. A ball that either rolls forward or sucks back makes it difficult to stop the ball pin high, because it adds another layer of judgment.

If you look at the sample Distance Wedge Matrix, you'll notice that the smallest backswing with a pitching wedge produces the lowest-trajectory, lowest-spinning shot, and a full swing with the most-lofted wedge produces the highest-trajectory shot with the most backspin. Within this matrix you can always hit two or sometimes three different clubs the same carry distance, but with completely different trajectories and spin rates. Picking the right shot, then, is nothing more than getting a feel for which shot will one-hop-and-stop on the green given the conditions (hard or soft greens, into the wind, off a downslope, etc.). Having this feel or sense is a skill that must be developed. It'll come with intelligent practice. Choosing the correct shot and the ability to add or subtract energy from your known numbers is the art of distance wedge play, and will allow you to outperform your old self and those around you.

Distance Wedge Strategy

Based on PGA Tour ShotLink data, your strategy should prioritize the following:

1. Laying up in the fairway.
2. Pushing the ball up as close to the green as is comfortable, as long as it doesn't involve unnecessary risks, bringing hazards into play, or losing quality position.

Obviously, there are situations when laying back to create more spin is the smarter play (tough pins on firm greens, playing downwind, etc.), but these are exceptions to the rule.

Process Is King

As with finesse wedges, the process of hitting and evaluating a shot needs to be more important than the shot itself. Define the process and own it. It should look something like this:

1. Assess the lie, the wind, and the quality position to the pin so you can identify a precise finishing target: *I want to stop this shot hole high but one yard left of the pin.*
2. Get the total yardage to that target: *It's 84 yards.*
3. Choose the club and shot that will one-hop-and-stop on the green: *It's a sand wedge.*
4. Given this shot and the conditions, announce the perfect carry number: *I'm going to carry it 80 yards.*
5. Adjust your perfect carry number to one that represents how far it will actually play given the conditions: *Because it's downhill and downwind, I think it'll play more like 74 yards.*
6. Get a plus or minus yardage relative to one of your known numbers with that club: *My nine o'clock shot carries 70 yards, so this is just four yards more.*
7. Pull your sand wedge and rehearse the feel of the shot. If you have a swing key based on a needed technique change, go ahead and focus internally and rehearse this key away from the ball. Internalize its feel and then put it in its proper place, which is nothing more than a gentle awareness from this point forward (awareness, not thought).
8. Face the target and visualize the shot you've chosen using external focus. Walk in clear to that picture, with 100 percent commitment to your strategy.
9. Address the ball.
10. See and do. "Tie your shoe." Trust. You've practiced hard and smart. The swing needed to produce a great shot is inside. Let it go.
11. If it's a good shot, embrace it. Show some emotion. Smile, if nothing else, and grow your S.I. If it's a poor shot, objectify it without emotion and ask yourself what the solution to that shot would be if you had a do-over. After becoming aware of it, replay it correctly in your mind and then be done. Self-coach in a positive way. View it as an opportunity to grow and to make the late, great John Wooden proud. This is something you can control!

JOURNAL WORK

Settle on a process that makes sense and is comfortable for you. Define every step of the process as I have above and write it down in the Distance Wedge section of your *Short Game Solution* journal. In your daily war to "feel like a champion," making process king is your opening salvo.

CHAPTER 14

DISTANCE WEDGE FLAWS AND FIXES

Much like a bunker shot, a distance wedge is more valuable to your score than just one shot. As such, consistent contact from 30 to 120 yards is critical; you can't afford debilitating misses if you want to score.

As I demonstrated in the last chapter, your distance wedge setup and swing largely mimic your full swing, with a few notable exceptions. And like all full swings, your distance wedge is complicated by a lot of moving parts. Despite its complexity, I've found that most distance wedge contact problems fall into four major categories, and that these common errors are relatively easy to fix. You just need to be able to identify them as problems, and to create a simple way to change your motor habits so that you can improve. Here's how.

DISTANCE WEDGE FLAWS AND FIXES

FLAW NO. 1: Taking too big of a backswing.

One of the great things about my wedge system is that is relies on shortening the backswing to reduce distance, which in itself solves one of the most common flaws that amateur players make. They take too big of a backswing for the desired distance and then intuitively quit as they come down, fearful that the ball will sail over the green. One mistake leads to another, and horrible contact and distance control are the results. A simple solution is to take the smallest backswing possible (while still hinging your wrists) to produce just enough energy to get the ball to the pin without losing rhythm. A smaller backswing encourages you to sequence correctly and to use your body to help deliver the club, which is essential for consistent contact and an optimal ball flight.

How you know you have it: You don't feel the urge to use your body to help finish the swing (because if you do, the ball will fly over the green).

Effect on angle of attack: Shallows it.

Effect on contact: Fat and thin shots.

How to fix it: Pause at your "benchmark."

> **Step 1:** On the range, tee up a ball just off the ground and address it using your distance wedge stance (slightly narrower, square feet, weight slightly favoring the lead foot, power grip).
>
> **Step 2:** Maintaining your weight throughout, swing your lead arm back to the nine o'clock position and pause. Turn your head and check that your lead arm is parallel to the ground (nine o'clock and no later).
>
> **Step 3:** Look back at the ball and then briskly swing through all the way to your finish line (the logo on your shirt, near your lead shoulder), clipping the ball off the tee. Note the distance that the ball travels. Complete five repetitions.
>
> **Step 4:** Repeat steps 2 and 3. This time, swing your lead arm back to the 7:30 position, or belly-button height. Remember to pause at the end of your backswing and complete your follow-through. Do five more repetitions, again noting the yardage.
>
> **Step 5:** Remove the tee and repeat both swings without pausing. Make sure you hit your benchmarks (7:30 or nine o'clock) so that you can use your body to deliver the club. Once you hit five solid shots with each swing, you're done.

FLAW NO. 2: Moving your center behind the ball.

Sound familiar? This is very similar to the situation in which energy moves away from the target in your finesse wedge swing and positions the low point of your swing arc behind the ball. Not good. The low point of your arc is basically the center of your mass, and you can't afford to move it behind the ball at any point. There are three common ways that players commit this fatal flaw.

Setting up improperly: If you have a wide stance and play the ball forward with your head back of center as if you're hitting a fairway wood, you're going to have difficulty creating solid contact with an abbreviated wedge swing. For distance wedge shots, narrow your stance, play the ball in the middle, and set up with 55 percent of your weight favoring your lead foot. This positions your head just slightly behind the ball. The narrow stance makes it easier to shift into your lead foot and finish your swing.

How you know you have it: You're looking at the back of the ball in your setup.

Effect on angle of attack: Shallows it.

Effect on contact: Fat and thin shots.

NO!
Wide stance.
Ball forward of center.
Head way behind the ball.

YES!
Narrower stance than your full swing.
Ball in the middle.
Weight slightly favoring lead foot.
Head barely behind the ball.

How to fix it: Make a "T."

> **Step 1:** Lay an alignment stick on the ground just inside the ball and parallel to the target line. Place a second stick even with the ball but perpendicular to the first stick, which will form a "T." This second stick should run directly between your feet and mark your ball position. Be sure to leave enough room between the second stick and the ball, because you're going to make a swing in this drill.
>
> **Step 2:** Using the alignment sticks as a guide, set your feet square to the first stick and no more than a foot apart from each other. Check that the second stick runs directly through the middle of your stance. Lastly, look down and position your head so that your nose is slightly behind the second stick.
>
> **Step 3:** Hit ten distance wedge shots, checking your setup to the "T" each time.

Shifting weight into your trail foot on the backswing: With your weight back, and given the shorter arm swing, there just isn't enough time to get it forward again to achieve an ideal impact position. Plus, it makes it difficult to flight down your wedge trajectory, which successful players typically do. Keeping your weight centered over the ball during the backswing—also known as "stacking"—makes this easy.

How you know you have it: You have trouble getting weight over to your lead side at impact.

Effect on angle of attack: Shallows it.

Effect on contact: Fat and thin shots.

NO!
Weight shifting to trail foot in the backswing.
Head drifting off the ball.

YES!
Balance slightly favoring the lead foot at address.
Balance maintained during the backswing.
Head remaining in the same position.

How to fix it: Use a stick.

Push an alignment stick into the ground on the side of the ball opposite your stance. Check that your weight is balanced or slightly favoring your lead foot. Look up; if your head is in the right position, the stick will be just in front of your lead ear. While looking at the stick, make a slow-motion backswing to the nine o'clock position and pause. Check that you're still balanced and that your head hasn't moved. Repeat five times. Hit five nine o'clock shots focusing solely on the feel of this drill.

Falling back: Shifting your weight to your trail foot on the downswing isn't allowed. Why? Hopefully you've got the point by now: Weight shifts forward in the wedge game. Always. If not, expect to hit behind the ball.

How you know you have it: You fall back on your trail foot in the finish.

Effect on angle of attack: Shallows it.

Effect on contact: Fat and thin shots.

NO!
Weight on trail foot at impact.
Head falling back.
Body rotation stalled out.

YES!
Lead hip and thigh shifting three to four inches toward the target.
Majority of weight on lead foot at impact.
Body turning through the ball.

How to fix it: Use the Right-Side-Passes-the-Left Drill (or vice versa for lefties).

STEP 1: Set up for a distance wedge shot (you don't need a ball). Take your lead hand off the grip and rest it on your lead hip, thumb pointing behind you. Make a trail-hand-only backswing and then gently swing through to a full finish.

STEP 2: You know that you've done it correctly if your trail shoulder, hip, and knee literally pass your lead hand in the direction of the target. The lateral and rotary body motion involved in correctly performing this drill trains your trail side to "cover the ball" as you near impact. This creates great contact and a lower, flighted trajectory. Hit the right finish position five times.

FLAW NO. 3: Delivering the club on a poor path.

Clubface angle and swing path through the ball work together to produce shot shape (along with angle of attack). Although the clubface can dramatically influence what path you swing on, when it comes to contact errors, swing path and angle of attack are the master variables. There's indeed a path "sweet spot" for optimal contact. Is your path too much out-to-in, in-to-out, or in the acceptable range? How would you know? Read on.

How you know you have it: You have difficulty starting the ball on line.

Effect on angle of attack: Out-to-in steepens it; in-to-out shallows it.

Effect on contact: Fat, thin, and off-center hits (even the shanks).

How to fix it: Try my Railroad Track Drill.

Lay two alignment sticks on the ground about five inches apart. Position them like railroad tracks pointing to the target, with the ball slightly shading the outside rail. There should be no more than a half-inch of clearance from the toe of the club to the outside stick, and one inch or so from the heel to the inside stick. Push several tees in the ground every three inches along the outside of both sticks to form a channel. Remove the sticks. The tees will provide a similar channeling effect without the risk of injury. (I've kept the sticks here for demonstration purposes only.)

Make one of your benchmark swings and deliver the club through the channel formed by the tees. If you hit a tee before or after impact, note the path error and make three slow-motion swings using the tees to both visualize and feel a more neutral path (i.e., straight down the tracks). After three successful slow-motion rehearsals, retest with another ball at regular speed. If you're successful at regular speed in the retest, groove that feel by making this drill a regular part of your block practice. If you fail at high speed (a 7-out-of-10 effort), do it with a 1-out-of-10 effort and gradually increase effort one increment level at a time. You're not going to be able to perform at a 7-out-of-10 effort if you can't first do it at 2, 3, 4, and so on. Repeat the process until you learn the feel for the movement required to consistently deliver the clubhead on a neutral path.

A Note on Path

The Railroad Track Drill paints a very clear story about your path. If you find yourself consistently striking the inside tees before you strike the ball, your delivery is too much from the inside-out. Prioritize the Right-Side-Passes-the-Left Drill in your block practice. If you tend to hit the outside tees before you strike the ball, you're delivering the club too much from the outside-in. In phase one of your downswing, make sure that your trail hip and chest remain closed as you move laterally toward the target, which will give your arms a chance to swing down the plane.

In any case, the first step is to diagnose the path error correctly (self-coaching), which is not that common. If I had a dollar for every time a student came to me with a hook miss telling me they were "coming over the top" when in fact their path was substantially in-to-out with the face closed to the target, I'd have enough money to buy after-round drinks for everybody. Note: swinging over the top contributes to either pulls or slices, while swinging in-to-out leads to pushes or hooks.

Many of the world's greatest players are able to hit perfect little draws or fades—the shot-control envy of the masses. They do it by shifting their path one way or the other and achieving a face angle at impact that's half as much open or closed as the path direction. For example, a perfect draw that lands in the cup may be represented by a path that's 4 degrees in-to-out with a face angle that's 2 degrees open to the target, yet 2 degrees closed to the path. I know it's counterintuitive that the face would need to be slightly open to the target for a perfect draw, but it's just physics—you can't argue it. What you're feeling on a draw is a face that's closed to the path, not the target.

FLAW NO. 4: Ignoring your swing verticals.

If you're struggling with contact and your divots are too deep, the Railroad Track Drill also has potential to help, because your path may be too far from out-to-in. If you can successfully execute the Railroad Track Drill but still suffer from fat shots with deep divots, then you need to focus on using your verticals.

How you know you have it: Your divots are too deep.

Effect on angle of attack: Steepens it.

Effect on contact: Fat shots and inconsistent distance control.

How to fix it: Go "slow-mo."

Step 1: Set up for a distance wedge swing (no ball necessary).

Step 2: In super-slow motion, rehearse the sequential movements of a fundamentally sound downswing. Start at the top:

- Shift laterally toward the target, allowing your arms to swing down in front of your belly. Pause. Transition to rotary body motion and deliver the club into the ball. As you do this, tap into the sensation of your lead leg straightening as the lead hip rotates back around toward your lead heel.
- Repeat, again in slow motion, this time tapping into the feel of your hand path flattening out and moving slightly upward, following the rotation of the lead shoulder up and around your head just prior to impact. Repeat steps 1 to 3 three times.

Learning to implement these swing verticals (steps 1 and 2, above) shouldn't take anything more than awareness. Shallower divots and a more controlled flight will be your reward.

JOURNAL WORK

Record your technical commitments for distance wedges and date your entry. Remember to define everything from setup keys to execution feels. Note the flaws and the prescribed drills or fixes that resonate. Use words that make sense to you.

DISTANCE WEDGES

MY DISTANCE WEDGE FEELS—SPRING 2015

Dropping My Arms.

Even though it's a power sequence, I need to be patient with the rotation at the start of my downswing. Doing the Railroad Track Drill showed me that when I rotate early I come from the outside.

WHEN I RECOGNIZE THIS MISS PATTERN.

Circle back and do the Railroad Track Drill!

FINISH!

Hitting my finish line is a constant—a variable that doesn't change. Shorten the backswing—not the finish—to make the ball go shorter.

CHAPTER 15

DISTANCE WEDGE
TRAINING PLAN

"It's not the will to win that matters—everyone has that. It's the will to prepare that matters."—Paul "Bear" Bryant

Mastering my Distance Wedge System requires the same structural practice mix as mastering finesse wedges and bunker shots: block training, random training, and game playing. Again, this formula provides an efficient blend of technique practice and skill development, and is only as effective as the effort you're willing to put into it. Remember, working hard and smart begins with paying attention to your intention. Regardless of what part of your distance wedge game you're focusing on, set a goal for each and every minute of your training.

DISTANCE WEDGE BLOCK TRAINING

Since distance control is the number-one key to high performance from distance wedge range, you'll need feedback regarding how far the ball carries in the air on every swing. Hopefully, your regular practice facility features clearly visible, marked targets from 120 yards and in. If not, you'll need to provide your own. All of my Tour players travel with small, stackable agility cones (available online and at most sporting good stores), which they use to mark specific yardages wherever their practice takes them. Items such as washcloths, alignment sticks, and the like will also do, as long as you can see them clearly at address. Don't place your markers haphazardly—you need to be precise. Investing in a quality range finder probably isn't a bad idea.

With your makers in place, warm up and hit several full-swing shots up to your 7-iron. Starting with your full swing allows you to feel your normal 9-out-of-10 swing effort, which is necessary to judge what your 7-out-of-10 effort feels like when you begin hitting distance wedges. After your full swing is warm, perform whatever drills you deemed necessary to improve your distance wedge swing when you were studying the flaws in the last chapter. Over time, the drills in your block practice may need to change as your swing naturally evolves. It shouldn't take more than ten swings to confirm that you're executing the fundamental involved with a specific drill correctly. And before you cave in to peer pressure and go back to making full swings with your 7-iron, keep in mind that distance wedge practice benefits your power game, too, since it involves performing the same type of swing.

After you complete your drills (limit them to two on a normal practice day), lay an alignment stick on the ground to simulate your target line (position it so it doesn't interfere with your swing). You'll never go wrong by working on aim. Plus, one of the major concepts within my systems is to commit to and master the little things such as aim and alignment. Select a wedge and execute five perfect shots with each of your benchmark swings (full, nine o'clock, and 7:30, or whatever you've decided to call them). Remember to lock in on your backswing length and a consistent 7-out-of-10 effort to your finish line. These fifteen swings will provide you with a feel for the swing you have that day and clues as to how the ball is behaving based on the environment (flying farther because you're at altitude or shorter because you're hitting into the wind). Once you confirm your known numbers using these swings, end your block practice. Again, this should take no more than ten minutes out of a typical thirty-minute practice session.

DISTANCE WEDGE SKILL DEVELOPMENT

After block practice, transition to random training using your full process and championship-feeling strategies. Recall that the purpose and intent of random practice is to develop your skill and judgment, in addition to solidifying your process. Play a variety of shots: low, high, fades, draws, etc. Owning the skill to hit a controlled, one-yard fade or draw on a distance wedge shot gives you a huge strategic advantage, and I'm a big fan of "holding your line in a crosswind" by curving the ball slightly against the wind's direction. Here's why: Imagine you have an 80-yard shot to a pin tucked on the right side of a green, and the wind is blowing from right to left. If you want to stop the ball as close to the pin as possible and "turn three shots into two," as Bobby Jones used to say, but you haven't developed the ability to hold your line with a little fade, your only strategic choice is to aim right of the pin (likely to a target that's actually off the green) and hope the wind blows the ball back toward the hole. This is a bad strategy for two reasons: 1) a ball that curves with the wind travels farther and hits the green with less spin, reducing your effective landing area and your ability to control the distance; and 2) it's not certain that the wind will blow the ball as expected, and you could end up missing the green to the right, leaving you with a short-sided, downwind finesse wedge. In either scenario, you're probably going to turn three shots into four. Developing the skill to shape distance wedge shots in random practice allows you to play like a pro in a crosswind and to start the ball on line and hold it there with a controlled fade. If executed correctly, the ball will appear to fly dead straight and then land softly on the green with normal, shot-stopping backspin.

Situations like these make this phase of training more interesting, especially when you're practicing from different distances to simulate what happens on the course. I use a random-number-generator (RNG) app on my smartphone that, as its name suggests, spits out random numbers within a range you define. I typically ask for ten to twenty random numbers and then work through each of them as if they're shots in an important tournament round using my full process, which is listed below:

- What's the number (total distance)?
- What club and shot is going to one-hop-and-stop?
- Where am I going to land the ball, and what's that number playing?
- What's the + or − from a known number with that club?
- Rehearse the feel of the swing for the shot and walk in clear and committed.
- Play the shot with external focus.
- Imprint or objectify. If the latter, make the correction and move on.

It's simple to do, but it takes more focus and discipline than the average player is willing to invest in a typical practice session. Do it on every shot. Don't be average!

End the random portion of your practice session by playing a game or two, testing both your skill and competitive spirit. I've listed several distance wedge specific games at the end of this chapter. The goal is to ramp up your intensity and focus in addition to learning how to execute with something on the line.

You want to win every day, so keep your definition of "winning" commensurate with your skill level.

I suggest playing a different game each practice session and setting a time limit of ten to fifteen minutes to complete it. The last thing you want to do is practice for too long, beating yourself up and losing confidence with each setback. When I play the game $30 Bank (see below), for example, I'll play it a second time if I run out of money, but I won't play it a third time if my results are the same. I'll move on to something else and accept that it just isn't my day, then think about what I have to do going forward to get as good as I want to be. Every player faces obstacles. Great players expect them, embrace the challenge they present, and can't wait to roll up their sleeves and break through them. Avoid being the guy who meets an obstacle and turns away thinking he doesn't have what it takes to move forward. Some things require a good measure of perseverance.

JOURNAL WORK

Armed with the information that I've given you about distance wedge block and random training, develop your own program and write it down in your journal. Start with block drills and confirm your known numbers. Practice in random mode as time allows, then end your training day with a game or two. Use your journal to chart your progress, saving space on the pages to note what you learned along the way. Meet obstacles head on and add action items to your plan to overcome them if necessary.

Block Practice		
ACTIVITY	QUANTITY/TIME	GOALS
Setup Checks	5 repetitions	Use a stick to confirm alignment and setup fundamentals.
Right-Side-Passes-Left Drill	5 perfect repetitions	Create the feeling of your trail side "covering" the ball through impact.
Benchmark Checks	Hit full, nine o'clock, and 7:30 benchmarks (for one club), 5 repetitions each	Create a baseline feel for the day. Get confirmation on yardage adjustments for the environment.

Random Practice		
ACTIVITY	QUANTITY/TIME	GOALS
Use an RNG to play twenty random shots. Use full process and all wedges. Play at least three draws and fades.	15 minutes	Develop judgment regarding shot selection, shapes, trajectory, and spin. Work on touch and feel as well as running your process.
Game Playing		
ACTIVITY	QUANTITY/TIME	GOALS
Play Three Trajectories Play Three Shapes Play $30 Bank	10 minutes	Compete and perform with simulated pressure and win your way off the wedge range.

INTENTFUL DISTANCE WEDGE PRACTICE GAMES

$30 Bank

On the practice range, choose a random number from 30 to 120. Select the appropriate club and swing to produce the same number in yardage, then hit the shot. Deduct $1 from an imaginary bank account with a balance of $30 for every yard you are off from the target. For example, if you're trying to hit a 90-yard shot and you come up three yards short and just a bit to the right so that the ball lands a total of four yards from the target, deduct $4, which leaves you with a balance of $26. See if you can hit ten random-distance wedges and still have money in the bank when you're done. My Tour students start with only $25. See if you can top that!

90-Yard 23

When the course is a little empty, head to a hole and play one ball all the way in, starting at 10 yards from the pin. On each hole repeat the process from a different 10-yard increment all the way up to 90. When you finish all nine holes, add up your strokes. A winning score is 23 or lower for a tournament-level player. Adjust according to your skill level, or set a goal score to inspire your competitive spirit.

Ten-Cone Birdie

On the practice facility, set up ten cones (or a marker of your choice) at 10-yard increments from 30 to 120 yards. Play a distance wedge to each cone in succession. Count the number of shots that land within two steps of the cones, or what I call "birdie range." Win your way off the practice facility by hitting seven shots to birdie range if you're a competition golfer, or five shots if you're a low-handicap amateur. Less-skilled players may go 0-for-10 at first. Set a goal based on your initial score and work to reach it.

Distance Wedge Knockout

Set eight cones (or markers) at 10-yard increments from 30 to 100 yards. Hit shots at the first cone until you land a ball within a two-yard radius (one yard for tournament-level players) of the target, which "knocks out" that distance. Proceed from cone to cone in order and in the same manner. Your Knockout score is the total number of balls it takes to knock out all eight cones. Try to set your personal scoring record each time you play, or match it using a smaller target radius.

Distance Wedge Six-Up

Challenge a player of similar skill level to a distance wedge shootout. Player A randomly selects a number and plays to that yardage, followed by Player B. Use the following scoring system:

    1 point for closest to the target.
    5 points for hitting the target on the fly.
    5 points for holing out on top of your competitor (who gets 0).

Player B chooses the next random yardage and hits first. The game continues in alternating order until one player gets six points ahead of the other, at which point the game is won.

Three Trajectories

Pick or set up a target. The goal is to land three shots within three yards of the target: a high-trajectory shot, a low-trajectory shot, and a normal-trajectory shot.

Your score is the total number of balls it takes you to successfully pull off all three shots. Play this game regularly, because it reminds you that you have trajectory options when you play. It also ensures that you train on all shots in practice, even the uncomfortable ones.

Three Shapes

Pick or set up a target. The goal is to land three shots within three yards of the target: a draw, a straight shot, and a fade. The lesson? Play shots, not swings. Your score is the total number of balls it takes you to successfully pull off all three shots.

PGA Tour Confidential: Kevin Chappell

"I'm a big believer that it takes more than having the right tools to get the job done. To get results, you need a plan that'll keep the tools sharp, or your hard work will mean nothing. With James's help, I've developed a practice routine that helps me sharpen my distance wedges, builds confidence, and allows me to measure the results. The process is the same for me every week. I don't rest on the work I've done in the past, because I play on different grasses and at different altitudes each week on Tour. It's critical for me to know my numbers and confirm my feels each event.

"Every Tuesday, my caddie sets up cones from 20 to 140 yards in 10-yard increments. I start each session with three to five shots to every cone. This warms up my body and gives me an idea on how far the ball is going. Once I've hit a few shots to every cone, I check my distances using my full, nine o'clock, and 7:30 benchmarks by hitting three good shots with each swing and each club.

"Once I have my distances for the week, my focus turns to competing. James and I have created games that I can play on the range that keep me engaged and challenged. My favorites are Three Shapes, Three Trajectories, and Ten-Cone Birdie.

"I've always had the tools, but James showed me how to keep them sharp and stay focused on my plan. As a result, both my confidence and skill have grown, and my distance wedge play has skyrocketed."

PARTING THOUGHTS

We cannot solve our problems with the same thinking we used when we created them.

—Albert Einstein

A coach's perspective and a player's perspective can be dramatically different. As a player, I remember how difficult it was to figure out what road to travel, and how easily doubt crept into my mind. After twenty-plus years of coaching, the road now seems so clear. There's a right way and a wrong way to go about getting better, and when I see players like Tom Pernice Jr., I.K. Kim, Ben Crane, Cameron Tringale, and Kevin Chappell (to name a few) demonstrate a commitment to going about it the right way, it steels my resolve and inspires me to share that message.

Many of you are stuck in the same performance quicksand that I labored in as a struggling Tour player—you're either working hard on the wrong things, or you're jumping from technique to technique hoping to hit upon the secret, all to no avail. The emotional toll of playing golf below your expectations is heavy. I want to spare you that burden.

I've put a lot of energy into helping many of the world's greatest players, but now it's about you. I'm your coach. And I'm asking you to use what you've read in this book to change your thinking, be disciplined, and commit to your plan. Can you envision yourself walking up to the ball six months from now with the swagger of Seve Ballesteros, knowing that you can produce a masterful shot in any situation? I can see it. I can also see your joy as you master the short game from 120 yards and in!

It's time for a new approach. It's time for *Your Short Game Solution*.